Philip Perring

The Spirit and the Muse

Original Hymns and Other Poems

Philip Perring

The Spirit and the Muse
Original Hymns and Other Poems

ISBN/EAN: 9783744777674

Printed in Europe, USA, Canada, Australia, Japan

Cover: Foto ©Thomas Meinert / pixelio.de

More available books at **www.hansebooks.com**

THE SPIRIT AND THE MUSE.

CHURCHES AND THEIR CREEDS.

By the REV. SIR PHILIP PERRING, Bart., late Scholar of Trinity College, Cambridge, Crown 8vo. 10s. 6d.

CONTENTS.

1. Conformists and Nonconformists.
2. A Precedent for the Bishops.
3. Regulation of Public Worship.
4. Expenses of Public Worship.
5. Episcopal Ordination.
6. Non-Episcopal Ordination.
7. The Baptismal Service.
8. Everlasting Damnation.
9. Biblical Revision.
10. Passages in the Gospels revised.
11. Gospel accounts of the Resurrection harmonized.
12. Silver Filings.

London: Longmans, Green, and Co., Paternoster Row.

"It is impossible not to commend the honesty, straightforwardness, and in many instances wholesomeness of his views."—*Sunday Magazine.*

"Language always thoughtful, and never offensive."—*Churchman's Shilling Magazine.*

"Much that is earnest, and, we think, well meant, in this volume."—*Christian Observer.*

"A vigorous book."—*Daily Telegraph.*

"It contains many good things."—*British Quarterly.*

"This book is another instance of the warning, so frequently given to the Church of England, of dangers arising from evils which it is in her own power to remove."—*The Rock.*

"When the author descends to particulars and gives us his views about matters of discipline and doctrine, we find ourselves for the most part in harmony with him."—*Spectator.*

"He thinks and writes with great freedom and vigour."—*Nonconformist.*

"He will not miss the mark for want of plain speaking."—*Standard.*

"He is thoroughly impartial as between Conformists and Nonconformists . . . . There are fair papers in the volume on the subjects of 'Episcopal Ordination,' and on the 'Baptismal Services' in the Church of England . . . . . . there is also a reasonably good paper on 'Everlasting Damnation' . . . . . . With respect to the Revision of the Authorized Version of the Scriptures, he gives us specimens of such a work in revised translations of some of the Epistles, which are done in a scholarly and temperate manner."—*Westminster Review.*

THE SPIRIT AND THE MUSE

CONTAINING

ORIGINAL HYMNS AND OTHER POEMS

WITH

TRANSLATIONS FROM THE ODES OF HORACE

BY THE

REV. SIR PHILIP PERRING, BART.

LATE SCHOLAR OF TRINITY COLLEGE, CAMBRIDGE,
AUTHOR OF "CHURCHES AND THEIR CREEDS."

"I will sing with the spirit, and I will sing with the understanding also."
1 COR. XIV. 15.

LONDON:
LONGMANS, GREEN, AND CO.
1872.

PREFACE.

To write a long Preface for a little book like the present would be to seem to claim for it a larger amount of attention than it is ever likely to obtain—perhaps, than it deserves. Nevertheless, the Author is not without a hope that it may find its way into the hands of some to whom it may prove both useful and interesting. There is an attractiveness in the Hymn that there is not in the Sermon, and a few short pieces of Sacred Poetry will often be relished where a continuous Discourse would be positively distasteful. I much doubt whether Clergymen, Heads of households, Superintendents of classes, and the like, are fully aware of the power for good that may be exerted by a free use of Hymns in their ministrations and services. Children are notoriously fond of them; the poor and illiterate listen to them gladly; invalids can bear this kind of literature when they can bear no other. Nor must it be forgotten that we have by no means yet a thoroughly good collection of Hymns for congregational use; every one who publishes a volume of Sacred Poetry may indulge the hope that from his, or her, volume may one day be drawn one or two pieces capable of exciting, or at least of expressing, the devotional feelings of thousands. In the matter of doctrine, if I have occasionally allowed myself a freer range than any one of the numerous sects, into which the Church of England is divided, would wittingly and willingly concede to its Ministers, I trust and believe that I have not overstepped those limits, which a careful study of Holy Scripture would lead us to conclude that the great Lord of the Universal Church has graciously marked out for us. I have a Hymn for those who are joined together in Holy Matrimony; a Hymn also for those who devote themselves to a religious life in cloister or nunnery. Perhaps, too, at a time when efforts are being made to induce the Clergy to desist from reading in the public services of the Church a Creed, so presumptuously precise in its definitions and distinctions, so daringly dogmatic in its sweeping denunciations, as the so-called Creed of St. Athanasius, my lines on the possible final restoration of the wicked may be read with somewhat more than a passing interest. But, whatever may be thought of my work as a whole, this at any rate must be conceded to me by every fair critic, that I have imitated no one's style, borrowed no one's ideas, pirated no one's expressions, appropriated no one's metres; my verses, such as they are, are *my own;* my sole sources of Inspiration have been the two great Volumes of God's Word and God's Works.

With respect to my translations from the Odes of Horace, I shall claim for them the merit of being fairly literal, and at the same time spirited. The Latin text, which for the convenience of the reader I have had printed alongside of the English version, I have taken from an edition of Horace by C. W. King and H. A. J. Munro, Fellows of Trinity College, Cambridge.

My thanks are due, and are now given, to the Society for Promoting Christian Knowledge for kindly permitting me to reprint from the *People's Magazine* some ten pieces, the copyright of which

I had transferred to them. Nor must I omit to thank an old friend, whose name I am not at liberty to mention, for many valuable hints, and much kind assistance afforded me in preparing this, as well as a former work, for the Press.

"𝔒 𝔏𝔬𝔯𝔡, 𝔣𝔯𝔬𝔪 𝔗𝔥𝔢𝔢 𝔦𝔰 𝔱𝔥𝔢 𝔓𝔬𝔴𝔢𝔯, 𝔱𝔬 𝔗𝔥𝔢𝔢 𝔟𝔢 𝔱𝔥𝔢 𝔤𝔩𝔬𝔯𝔶."

CONTENTS.

PREFACE ... ... v.

PART I.
ORIGINAL HYMNS AND OTHER POEMS.

	PAGE.
To the Critic	1
The Choirs of Heaven	1
Holy Matrimony	3
Taking the Veil	5
Holy Communion	7
Holy Baptism	9
The Carrying Angel and the Departed Spirit	11
The Spirits in Prison	14
The Churchyard	18
The House of Mourning	19
Missionary Hymn	21
Good Words and Comfortable Words	23
The Christian Sabbath	25
The House of God	27
The Word of God	29
Watchnight	31
The Close of the Year	33
The New Year	35
Morning	38
The Night-watches	40
Peace	41
St. Michael and All Angels	42
The Invisible Presence	44

CONTENTS.

	PAGE.
The Love of God	47
Christmas	49
The Shepherds of Bethlehem	51
The Sufferings of Jesus	53
Witnesses of the Resurrection	55
Jesus the Life of the World	57
Praise to the Lamb	59
Trusting in the Lord	61
A Better Country	62
Spiritual Groanings	64
Whitsuntide	66
Dull Ears, Hard Hearts	68
Jesus the Light of the World	70
Stilling the Tempest	72
The Godly Man	74
Repentance from Dead Works	75
Confession of Sin	76
The Tale of our Sins	78
Christian Wisdom	79
Prayer	81
The Imperfection of our Prayers	84
The Blessed of the Lord	85
The Blood of the Atonement	87
The Blessedness of Poverty	88
Ill-gotten Wealth	91
Almsgiving	93
Divine Treasure	95
Waiting for our Change	96
Heavenly Rest	98
Life in the Wilderness	100
The Christian Soldier	102
Christian Watchfulness	104
The Christian Pilgrim's Progress	106
The Comfort of Sufferings	108

CONTENTS.

	PAGE.
The most Holy Place	110
The Living and the Dead	112
The Trees of Eden	114
The Fallen Tree	116
Culture of the Soul	120
The River of Life	122
The Southern Cross	124
The Lilies	126
Rain from Heaven	128
Living Waters	130
The Fatherland	132
The Temple of the Lord	134
Good Fruits	140
Life from the Dead	141
Seed-time and Harvest	142
The Tares	143
The Trees of the Wood	145
The Leaves of the Wood	147
The Saviour and the Sinner	148
A Sacrifice for Sin	150
Cruelty to Animals	151
The Good Shepherd	154
The Fishers	156
The Promise of the Father	158
Spiritual Utterances	159
Signs of the Times	161
Hope amid Billows	163
The Carcase-vultures	165
The Last Judgment	170
The Prince of Wales in a Court of Justice	180
Recovery from Sickness of the Prince of Wales	182
National Thanksgiving for the Recovery	184
Marriage of the Princess Louise and the Marquis of Lorne	186
The University Boat-race	189

xii. CONTENTS.

	PAGE
The Demon of War	190
France and Prussia	191
The Instability of Earthly Greatness	192
The Reds of Paris	194
Reformation	196
On the Death of Sir Charles Clarke	198
The Days of our Age	201
Epitaph on a Poor Man	202
The Power of God	204
The Steam-engine	205
The News of the Day	206
On the Death of Bishop Philpotts	207
Translation of a Latin Epigram	207

PART II.

TRANSLATIONS FROM THE ODES OF HORACE.

	PAGE
Book I.—Ode I.	211
Ode XI.	215
Ode XIV.	217
Ode XV.	221
Ode XXIV.	227
Ode XXXIV.	231
Book II.—Ode XVI.	235
Ode XVIII.	241
Book III.—Ode XVI.	245
Ode XVIII.	251
Ode XXIII.	255
Ode XXIX.	259
Book IV.—Ode VII.	267
Ode VIII.	271
Epode I.	275
Epode II.	279
The End	286
Index	287

PART I.

ORIGINAL HYMNS AND POEMS.

TO THE CRITIC.

Think not, O man who dost this book review,
I fancy all within is good and new,
Much it contains has been already said,
And may perchance be elsewhere better read;
Much you may deem lacks the authority
Of the great Doctors of Divinity,
Yet, as in Nature search is not in vain
In a large chaff-heap for some golden grain—
As, when we ramble on the pebbly shore,
We now and then pick up a madrepore,
So doubtless in these pages you will find
Some matter good and precious of its kind;
That much—my Christmas gift—set down as gain;
What's left—the refuse . . . . suffer to remain.

THE SPIRIT AND THE MUSE.

THE CHOIRS OF HEAVEN.

"Singing and making melody in your heart to the Lord."

The music of the Heavenly spheres
Is not like that which strikes our ears
   In this our poor abode,
But richer finer harmonies
The spirits sing in Paradise
   Before the throne of God:

Yet from the heart of earthly saint
Sounds of sweet music, though but faint,
   As from some lowly shrine,
May mingle with the melody
Of Heaven's Angelic company,
   Pleasing the ear divine;

THE SPIRIT AND THE MUSE.

If only God, who liketh well
Within the humble heart to dwell,
    Will set the chords aright,
That this poor broken instrument
May sound a sweet accomp'niment
    Meet for the Sons of Light.

HOLY MATRIMONY.

"What God hath joined together, let not man put asunder."

Rejoice, ye nuptial twain,
Bound by a mystic chain,
Fair is the marriage love
Which God has sealed above.

Daughter, who now art wed
To this thy lord and head,
Let not the serpent's guile
Thy simple mind defile.

Son, in God's image made,
Love thou this holy maid,
And be the strength and guide
Of her, thy chosen bride.

Let no unseemly strife
Break out 'twixt man and wife,
Hallow the earthly tie
By Heavenly harmony.

Observe the solemn troth
Here witnessed by you both—
One mind, one soul, one heart,
One *faith*, till death shall part.

God grant you rich increase!
God grant you joy and peace!
And at the last to rest
For ever with the blest!

TAKING THE VEIL.

"That ye may attend upon the Lord without distraction."

Virgin daughter, who art led
To this altar to be wed,
Who thy heart and soul hast given
Freely to the God of Heaven,

Christ thy husband thou dost choose,
Christ thy love will not refuse;
Thou shalt be his holy bride,
He shall be thy Lord and Guide:

Clad in raiment white as snow,
None more beautiful than thou;
Faithfulness, and truth divine,
Spotless purity, are thine.

Hark! a thousand thousand times
Sound the everlasting chimes;
Angels, unperceived by men,
Throng the glorious wedding train.

Virgin daughter, from this hour
Know the Heavéns are thy dower;
Earth has nothing to compare
With the glories treasured there.

Lowly, lowly, lowly bow,
Ere thou take the solemn vow;
Then to earth *for ever* dead,
Then to Christ *for ever* wed.

HOLY COMMUNION.

" Ye do shew the Lord's death till he come."

A spotless Lamb, by God's command,
    Was on the Jewish altar slain,
That men might know that blood alone
    Could take away the sinner's stain;

But none, save Jesus, God's own Son,
    Could cleanse from sin, or stop the curse;
His body broken, blood poured forth,
    Redeemed the guilty Universe:

The work he finished: now no more
    Jesus himself is offered up,
Yet still, in thankful memory,
    We break the bread, and take the cup;

And, as in love and joy and peace
　His people in communion meet,
They hail by faith that better feast,
　When Christ himself with them shall eat.

O Lord, thy dying love exceeds
　What men or angels can declare;
Teach us, while here thy death we shew,
　For thy bright presence to prepare.

HOLY BAPTISM.

"He took them up in his arms, put his hands upon them, and blessed them."

Mother, with thy precious load,
Standing by the Font of God,
Know that Jesus did of old
Infants in his arms enfold;
Know that he their surety stood,
Shedding his atoning blood:
He, who died the world to save,
Wills this little one to have.
See the water, God's own sign,
By the word, of grace divine;
Calling on the Holy Name,
For thy babe the blessing claim;
We will drop the Heavenly dew,
God will form the soul anew;

Then, upon the infant's face
As the Saviour's cross we trace,
Pray we that, when called to drink
Of His cup, he may not shrink.
Heirs of glory! heirs of bliss!
Such the children who are his;
He will help them through the fight,
Crown, and give them robes of white;
When the Lord the dead shall raise,
Babes shall rise to give him praise:
Now to God the Father be,
And, Eternal Son, to thee
Blessing, glory, honour, power,
Through all ages evermore.

THE CARRYING ANGEL AND THE DEPARTED SPIRIT.

"I heard a voice from Heaven saying unto me, Write, Blessed are the dead which die in the Lord from henceforth: yea, saith the Spirit, that they may rest from their labours, and their works do follow them."

ANGEL *speaks:*

" Hail, Spirit, last from earth,
But not of mortal birth,
Well hast thou run,
Thy labour now is done,
Thy life in Heaven's begun;
Put on thee now this robe of Heavenly white,
And be for ever now a child of light,
Standing in great Jehovah's sight."

SPIRIT *answers :*

O bright ! O best abode !
To rest at last with God !
    Expected long,
Much sought in prayer, in song,
Days, nights, and years, how long !
Exceeding expectation ! far above
Where fancy in her highest flight could rove !
Well worth the toil ! God's gift of love !

ANGEL :

It is as thou hast said,
And well art thou repaid
    All thou did'st dare
    Bravely to do and bear ;
    Answered in full thy prayer ;
But not one millionth part dost thou yet know
Of what Almighty goodness will bestow
    On thee—on *all* who loved below.

THE SPIRIT AND THE MUSE.

SPIRIT:

Great love ! transcending thought !
Who first us sinners bought
With Jesus' blood,
Then made us like to God,
Now gives us this abode,
Where, were we endless ages to remain
Just as we are, what lack? who could complain,
Seeing with God, as kings, we reign ?

ANGEL :

'Tis so : supremely blest
Whose lot is here to rest ;
And now farewell :
What God shall will, is well ;
It is not mine to tell
The countless worlds, where countless myriads raise
To the great Father everlasting praise
For all his great and wondrous ways.

THE SPIRITS IN PRISON.

"He went and preached unto the spirits in prison, which sometime were disobedient, when once the long suffering of God waited in the days of Noah."

Alas the lost—the dear,
We long since laid upon their bier,
    Then saw no more!
They lived, they died, in sin;
How could God's holy Angels take them in
    Th' eternal door?

    For them a dreadful doom—
Their bodies in the silent tomb
    Crumbled to dust;
And in a place below
Th' avenging Angels did their souls bestow:
    Their doom was just.

SPIRIT:

Great love! transcending thought!
  Who first us sinners bought
    With Jesus' blood,
  Then made us like to God,
  Now gives us this abode,
Where, were we endless ages to remain
Just as we are, what lack? who could complain,
  Seeing with God, as kings, we reign?

ANGEL:

  'Tis so : supremely blest
  Whose lot is here to rest;
    And now farewell :
  What God shall will, is well;
  It is not mine to tell
The countless worlds, where countless myriads raise
To the great Father everlasting praise
  For all his great and wondrous ways.

THE SPIRITS IN PRISON.

"He went and preached unto the spirits in prison, which sometime were disobedient, when once the long suffering of God waited in the days of Noah."

Alas the lost—the dear,
We long since laid upon their bier,
Then saw no more!
They lived, they died, in sin;
How could God's holy Angels take them in
Th' eternal door?

For them a dreadful doom—
Their bodies in the silent tomb
Crumbled to dust;
And in a place below
Th' avenging Angels did their souls bestow:
Their doom was just.

Alas! we mourned them sore,
While lasted yet their Life's brief hour;
    They would not hear:
  Have we no tears to shed,
Now they are suffering in that prison dread?
    They *still* are dear.

    What! may we sympathize
With those who dying closed their eyes
    Foes of God's power?
  Is it not now too late?
Must we not own the justice of their fate,
    And love no more?

    O God, tis hard to break,
E'en when we do it for thy sake,
    With those we love:
  Such love for thee below
We feeble creatures cannot fully show—
    We may *above*.

What if we see again
Those sinners dear without a stain
    Of sin and death!
    O God, thy mighty power
After their prison-penance can restore
    The living breath.

    How can we disbelieve
What thou, who never canst deceive,
    Thyself hast said,
    How Jesus from the grave
The word of Life to deluged sinners gave,
    Our King and Head?

    Then may not ours be glad,
As, musing in their chambers sad,
    They think of One,
    Who went himself to Hell,
And did of old the cheering tidings tell
    Of Victory won?

And may not we rejoice
That they may hear his kindly voice,
And see his face?
Then shall those dead trees bloom,
The quickened spirits come forth from the tomb,
Praising God's grace.

For a fuller exposition of the doctrine suggested in this Hymn see the chapter headed " Everlasting Damnation," in a little work entitled " Churches and their Creeds," published by Messrs. Longmans, Green, and Co., Paternoster Row, London.

THE CHURCHYARD.

" He giveth his beloved sleep."

Let not the rude unhallowed sound
Of riot mirth be heard around
The still Churchyard, whose chambers keep
Their bodies who have fall'n asleep;

The Lord has called them to their rest;
God grant their spirits may be blest,
And, at the great day of release,
They may enjoy eternal peace!

Pause, then, and breathe a silent prayer
O'er those who lie sepultured here,
That God may grant with them to *thee*
A glorious immortality.

THE HOUSE OF MOURNING.

" Sorrow not, even as others which have no hope."

Mourner, weep! To shed the tear
For the friends we hold most dear,
Though they may not see or hear,
Is indeed a comfort here:
But remember, Jesus said,
When the widow's hopes had fled,
" Weep not."—At his word the dead
Woke, and left the funeral bed.

Mourner, weep! But know that thou
Canst not 'scape the common woe;
In a few short years or so,
We shall be as those below:
Yet we need not moan our fate,
Be it early, be it late;
Christ, who burst th' infernal gate,
For his coming bids us wait.

Mourner, weep! But in the day,
When the Creature of decay
Shall put on his bright array,
What, O mourner, wilt thou say?
When the saints their Lord shall meet,
Friends long-parted friends shall greet,
All enjoy communion sweet
In the heavens, their lasting seat!

MISSIONARY HYMN.

"Go, ye swift messengers."

High blows the wind, and strong the gale,
Which fills the mission vessel's sail;
Go forth, ye noble spirits, go,
The Lord himself stands at the prow,
The Lord will speed you on your way,
Your guide by night, your guide by day,
Till ye shall reach th' appointed bay.

'Tis not for gold ye're sailing o'er
The mighty ocean's deafening roar;
'Tis not that ye would fain disown
Your native land for lands unknown;
'Tis not to view with rapt'rous eyes
The splendid landscape, splendid skies
Of some far distant Paradise:

A nobler motive prompts your quest,
A holier purpose fills your breast;
Moved by the Spirit from above,
Yours is a voyage full of love;
The bread of life ye take to feed
The famished nations in their need;
Well, Christian merchants, may ye speed!

GOOD WORDS AND COMFORTABLE WORDS.

" My brethren, be strong in the Lord, and in the power of his might."

Men, brothers bold,
To sin and Satan sold,
Bear not to be the thralls
Of him whose bondage galls;
Know, Christ for you has died,
And broke th' oppressor's pride;
His subjects be,
Rally beneath his banner, and be free.

What! still remain,
And hug the deadly chain!
Shall prisoners refuse
The freedom they may choose?
Shall Christ in vain have shed
His blood for souls so dead?
Arm for the strife,
Do battle for your liberty—your Life.

Brothers, make haste,
The precious time ye waste;
Each moment that ye stay
Adds danger to delay;
Begin at once the fight,
Strong in the Lord your might;
Arise, before
The voice which calls is hushed, to call no more.

Come, join th' array,
There's glory in this fray,
Already in the war
Jesus is conqueror;
Before the Prince of light,
See! darkness takes its flight:
To him be power,
And glory, and dominion, evermore.

THE CHRISTIAN SABBATH.

"This is the day which the Lord hath made, we will rejoice and be glad in it."

Who that has watched the billows roll,
Or eyed the wonders of the pole,
Or seen the lightning rend the sky,
Or heard the thunder rolling by,
Or marked throughout the circling year
The seasons each its produce bear,
Or mused in holy solitude
On what is just and true and good,
But knows that *man* is not alone,
But cared for by th' Almighty One,
Who would his creatures should be blest
With holy work and holy rest;
But chiefly on the Sabbath day
May we discern the better way;

For then did he, who died for men,
Jesus our Saviour, rise again,
And open out to mortal sight
New realms of undiscovered light:
Then cease this day from worldly care,
And give thyself to praise and prayer,
And tell abroad the gracious plan,
How God redeemèd sinful man.

THE HOUSE OF GOD.

" A tabernacle for a shadow."

The mercy of the Lord as far exceeds
All human mercies, as bright flowers do weeds,
Enlivening ever with a constant bloom
This desert world, these skies o'ercast with gloom.

Thy temples, Lord, are like a hallowed bower,
Wherein thy weary pilgrims rest an hour,
There, in their journey heavenwards, to be fed
By angel-hands with Christ, the living bread.

What joy is theirs, to pause, though but a while,
And join in holy converse without guile,
To praise thee for the wonders of thy hand,
And pray for strength to reach the better land!

Refreshed and strengthened, soon again they rise
To brave the dangers of their enterprise,
Looking for Christ, their Saviour-King, to come
Himself, and take them to their promised home.

THE WORD OF GOD.

"When thy word goeth forth, it giveth light and understanding unto the simple."

We give thee thanks, O Lord,
For thy most holy Word;
O write upon our hearts
The truths which it imparts:

Dispose us day by day
Its precepts to obey,
And grant, the more we know,
The holier we may grow.

What here we cannot see
But most imperfectly,
Teach us by faith to prize
As highest mysteries.

The stars of heaven shall fail,
The sun and moon grow pale,
Thy Word, O Lord, divine
Shall more than ever shine.

O let the gladd'ning light.
Dawn on the realms of night,
And to the world proclaim
The great Messiah's name.

WATCHNIGHT.

"This year also."

CHORUS OF VOICES.

" O take him away !   O take him away !
" He's a child of the night and not of the day!
" O take him away ! "

ANOTHER CHORUS.

" We plead for this sick and drooping soul,
" O pardon his sin and make him whole!
" O make him whole ! "

Such were the voices I seemed to hear
Just at the close of the dying year,
Spirits in conflict, these for my death,
Those to prolong yet awhile my breath.

Thousands of Seraphim loud and long
Sing round the throne of God their song,
Yet doth the faintest whisper of prayer
Pierce through His ear, who sitteth there:
Methought that in mercy he heard the prayer
Of those who besought him my life to spare!
Straightway there flew from the realms on high
One of those Cherubs that fill the sky;
Cleansed was my soul from sin's foul stain,
Snatched was my soul from Satan's reign,
Strengthened with Heaven's refreshening dew,
I fell on my knees and prayed anew:

> For every prayer which I lifted on high,
> For every bitter repentant sigh,
> For every struggle, hearty and true,
> To forsake my sin, and my duty do,
> For every cross I bravely endured,
> For every success by grace secured,

Thousands of saints, who had fought and won,
Methought I heard crying, "Well done! Well done!"

THE CLOSE OF THE YEAR.

"Hide thy face from my sins, and blot out all mine iniquities."

O Lord, I pray thee to efface
For ever every sinful trace,
Which thine all seeing eye can see
Clearly in every part of me.

Let thy most precious blood atone
For all the evil I have done,
And grant that I may never be
A castaway, good Lord, from thee.

Let not the God of this world blind
And hold in unbelief my mind,
But fix my heart on things above,
And let me see and know thy love.

Teach me to spend each passing year,
Rememb'ring thou art ever near,
Striving in all things to fulfil
With all my heart thy perfect will;

That, when I have fulfilled the span
Thou metest out to mortal man,
I may through mercy have a place
With those who see thee face to face.

THE NEW YEAR.

"The time is near."

Another year has past,
   Time and the world yet last,
Not yet has Jesus come
   To take his people home.

Ye holy men, endure,
   Your confidence is sure;
Though wickedness wax strong,
   It shall not be for long,

A little while, and then
   Jesus shall come again,
To give to each his due—
   Judgment most just and true.

When Jesus comes to reign,
   The world—ah! *then* how vain
Seek ye no earthly prize,
   Lift to the heavens your eyes.

Despise the toil and shame,
   Your Lord endured the same;
Stand fast and persevere,
   The time is drawing near.

To be with Jesus then,
   Like Angels, not like men!
Such glory to attain
   Were worth a little pain.

Ye who are waxing faint,
   Make to the Lord complaint;
Strive but to do his will,
   He will preserve you still.

Ye who have gone astray,
   Lo! Jesus is the way;
Ye who are sore opprest,
   Lo! Jesus offers rest.

O heed the gracious call
  Of him who died for all,
Now is the day of grace,
  Now seek the Saviour's face.

One universal cry
  Be raised to God on high
For safety in the strife,
  For the all-glorious Life.

MORNING.

"How long wilt thou sleep, O sluggard?"

Long since has the orient Sun
Through the heavens his course begun,
Cheering with his glorious ray
This fair world another day:
Now the bee is on his road,
Now the ant has got her load,
Now the beasts, though wild and rude,
Have by search obtained their food;
Wherefore, man, with sluggard head
Dost thou turn upon thy bed?
Up, and use the precious time;
Lo! Creation's in its prime.

Now the dew is on the grass,
Now the lake is clear as glass,
Now the earth, refreshed with showers,
Yields her sweetest loveliest flowers;
Now the birds are on the wing,
Now their cheeriest songs they sing;
Listen to the whispering breeze,
Listen to the rustling trees;
Nature bids thee, man, awake,
Nature for thy teacher take;
Up, and use the precious time,
Lo! Creation's in its prime.

God, who gave thee thy domain,
Bade thee, when he made thee, reign;
Beasts and cattle need their Head.
Rouse thee, sluggard, from thy bed:
Wherefore tarry? Art thou loth?
Is thy soul o'ercome with sloth?
Up, and let thine incense rise
To the Sovereign of the skies;
Join thy voice in praise and prayer
With Creation for his care;
Then to labour—now's the time;
Lo! Creation's in its prime.

THE NIGHT WATCHES.

" I sleep, but my heart waketh."

The sun is sinking in the west,
The labourer's hast'ning home to rest,
The beast to lair, the bird to nest;
To watch and pray, O man, is best.

The Angels, ne'er weighed down with sleep,.
In heaven eternal vigil keep;
Oh! in the hour of darkness deep
Rejoice, ye saints, ye mourners, weep.

Now cleanse the soul from earthly soil,
Now fill the lamp with holy oil,
Now the great Tempter's projects foil,
Lest of the heart he make a spoil.

PEACE.

"There was no more sea."

Restless the waves of human passions swell
Over the vast expanse of earth's domains,
Never to cease, while earth itself remains
    With heaven and hell:

But when earth, heaven, and hell shall pass away,
Then has the Lord ordained with them shall cease
This angry tumult, and instead, the peace
    Of endless day.

ST. MICHAEL AND ALL ANGELS.

"He shall give his Angels charge concerning thee."

In the dark night, when all is still,
    And men are wrapt in sleep,
Angels, performing God's high will,
    Watch o'er the holy keep:

With silent motion through the air
    Unnoticed they descend,
They seek not empty homage here,
    God's glory is their end.

The sick, the wounded in the strife,
    The faint, the sore distrest—
To these they whisper words of life
    And dreams of holy rest.

At early dawn with gentle hand
    They break the calm repose,
And onward cheer the pilgrim band
    Through all earth's toils and woes.

Grant, Lord, that, when life's day shall end,
    And death's dark night is come,
Thy Angel-guards may still attend
    To bear our spirits home.

THE INVISIBLE PRESENCE.

"And he said, Thou canst not see my face, for there shall no man see me, and live."

What holy secret, Lord, is this,
That thou dost ever round us dwell?
The earth, the heaven, hell's dark abyss
The greatness of Thy presence tell.

Our thoughts, our ways, our heart's desire,
Our purpose hid, our plans exprest,
Our words, our looks, our life entire,
All, all to Thee are manifest.

At home, abroad, awake, asleep,
With others, or companionless,
In daylight broad, in darkness deep,
Thou'rt present, God of holiness.

No voice we hear, no form we see,
Nor mighty sign, nor miracle,
Yet still, in awful majesty,
Thou'rt present, Great Invisible.

Amazing thought! that God most high
Should stoop so low, should be so near!
On this vile earth should cast his eye!
Should us poor sinners hold so dear!

Ah! not to judge—'tis to bestow
Gifts far exceeding, Lord, our due,
That Thou dost walk with us below,
Albeit hidden from our view:

And if the sight of Thee's concealed
From these dim eyes, 'tis only till
The sin-sick soul by grace is healed,
And sight of God would bring no ill.

For scarce we bear the sun's bright rays,
Or the quick lightning's awful might;
How then could we endure the blaze
Of the Creator's glorious light?

O never could the sinner's eye
Behold the Godhead and not die :
Come, then, we pray thee, come, Lord, nigh,
But come to us invisibly.

THE LOVE OF GOD.

"God is love."

High in the heavens above
  Dwells the great God of love,
We in this earth beneath
  Were heirs of sin and death;

But the great God of love
  Sent his Son from above,
And by his living breath
  Saved us from sin and death:

Therefore no longer now
  Is our life here below,
But in the heavens above,
  Where dwells the God of love;

And like him we shall grow
  More and more here below,
Till again he in love
  Sends his Son from above:

What *then* our life shall be,
  We know not; only He—
The Lord in whom we trust—
  We *know* is good and just.

CHRISTMAS.

"A babe lying in a manger."

Think not that babe, so weak and small,
   Thou seest in yonder cattle-stall.
Is, like the most of human race,
   Destined for some inglorious place:

Hid by a veil of flesh, behold
   The Christ, whom prophets have foretold,
Come now at last, the world to save
   From sin, from Satan, and the grave.

His holy empire shall extend
   Throughout the earth from end to end,
Throughout vast regions of the sky
   Unviewed as yet by mortal eye:

Therefore it was that shepherds came
　To see the babe of Bethlehem ;
Therefore the wise men from afar
　Followed the leading of the star ;

Therefore all Christian people raise
　From year to year glad hymns of praise
To him, who, though high Lord of all,
　Was born and cradled in a stall.

Man of the world, headstrong and wild,
　Despise not thou this heavenly child ;
If thou hereafter would'st be great,
　Thine too must be a low estate.

THE SHEPHERDS OF BETHLEHEM.

"The shepherds returned glorifying and praising God."

When Christ was born and laid
In a rude manger-bed,
Poor shepherds of the fold
Were first the tidings told :
From heaven a glorious light
Shone through the dark of night.
And Angels from above
Sang out the Father's love ;
Heaven heard the joyful cry,
Earth gave the glad reply :
" Glory to God in highest realms be given,
" Peace upon earth, good will to men from heaven."

Scarce had the Angels gone,
The shepherds every one
Set out to see the sign
Of him of David's line;
With utmost speed they came
That night to Bethlehem;
They saw him in the stall,
A babe, the Lord of all;
They told the listening crowd
What Angels sang aloud,
And much the people wondered at the word,
But Mary mused the more, the more she heard.

No gifts those holy men
Took to their folds again;
No rich and sumptuous fare
Broke for a while their care;
The cold and dewy night—
The stars to give them light—
A weary watch to keep
Over a flock of sheep—
Poor shepherds still, the same
As when the Angels came;
Yet, as from Bethlehem they homeward went,
They praised the Lord their God, and were content.

THE SUFFERINGS OF CHRIST.

"Thinkest thou that I cannot now pray to my Father, and he shall presently give me more than twelve legions of angels?"

The armies of the heavenly hosts
Stand watching at their several posts,
Ready to draw the glittering sword,
If great Jehovah speak the word.

Ah! wherefore then is God's own Son
In hour of darkness left alone,
Betrayed, condemned, led forth to die
A robber's death on Calvary?

Such was th' Almighty Father's will
To save the world from deadly ill;
For *us* the willing victim bled,
For *us* was numbered with the dead.

A full atonement now is made,
The sumless debt of sin is paid,
The Grave is conquered, man is free,
We live, we live eternally.

WITNESSES OF THE RESURRECTION.

"Him God raised up, and showed him openly, not to all the people, but unto witnesses chosen before of God."

Ask we the cause so few,
The Lord of life who knew,
Beheld him, when from death he rose to view—
 The holy women, then
 A group of faithful men,
And last in Galilee a humble train:

Know, this was God's own way,
By which, his wrath to stay,
He proved if men would listen and obey:
 Not in the people's sight,
 Not in his risen might,
Not with a sudden blaze of heaven-sent light—

In silent power arose
From his three days' repose
The Lord, the Saviour, startling friends and foes;
    He stood in flesh and bone,
    Seen but by few, alone,
Himself the witness that the work was done!

    He, who did thus appear
    Of old in vision clear
To those who did in humble faith draw near,
    Has promised to send down
    His Spirit to his own,
Till he shall come *Himself*, their joy and crown.

JESUS THE LIFE OF THE WORLD.

"The Life was manifested."

Jesus, for ages long concealed,
Jesus, whom God the Father sealed,
Jesus, our Life, is now revealed!

They laid him in a manger-bed,
They crowned with thorns his holy head,
They took him to the tomb when dead.

Now, seated on a heavenly throne,
He wears an everlasting crown,
And Death and Hell has trampled down.

In every place, the world around,
As men tell out the joyful sound,
Blessings increase and joys abound.

Angels and saints, fall down before
Jesus, our Life, in this his hour
Of glory and Almighty power.

PRAISE TO THE LAMB.

" Worthy is the Lamb that was slain."

Worthy to live and reign
The Lamb who once was slain,
Worthy of honour, worship, power,
From *all* for evermore.

'Tis he who intercedes
For us in all our needs,
'Tis he who, when we faint with fear,
Sends down the Comforter.

'Tis he who leads his own
By paths to them unknown,
That he may give them an abode
For ever with their God.

O help us, Lord, we pray,
Help us in this our day,
That, when in glory thou appear,
We may that glory share.

TRUSTING IN THE LORD.

" Trust ye in the Lord alway."

Those, only those, are truly blest,
Who in the Lord Jehovah rest,
Not seeking in a world like this
A false and transitory bliss.

Reserved for faith's triumphant band
Are lasting joys in that fair land,
Whither the Lord has gone before,
That we may go, when life is o'er.

There let us fix our steadfast eyes
Far from all earthly vanities;
Short is our life; this evening's ray
May mark the dawn of endless day.

A BETTER COUNTRY.

"Here have we no continuing city but we seek one to come."

In days of trial and distress,
When none can aid or give redress,
When hearts are cold and hopes are wan,
And fear comes over every man,
How sweet it is to know there is
A happier holier world than this,
A world no foe, nor pain, nor pest,
Nor sin, nor sorrow can molest,
Which they who reach can never cease
To live in love and joy and peace—
To know, too, that the Lord who bore
For us the Cross has gone before,
Has passed within those heavenly doors,
That we might know that world is ours—
To know that in a few short days,
If we but ponder well our ways,

We may indeed ourselves belong
To that most high most holy throng ;
Nor fable this, nor idle dream,
Nor as the things which merely seem ;
This is the Word which God has given,
This is the truth brought down from heaven ;
When God alone with Christ shall reign,
This Word of Truth shall still remain.

"SPIRITUAL GROANINGS."

"Even we ourselves groan within ourselves, waiting for the adoption, to wit, the redemption of our body."

While yet on earth
To feel the throbbings of the heavenly birth—
To rise above the turmoil and the strife
Of this most troubled life—
Calmly to rest
Upon the Saviour's breast,
Submissive to the Father's wise behest—
What purer bliss
To earthly saint than this?

Soon to the brink
Of this terrestrial world again we sink;
Our fleshly fetters will not let us soar
    Long on the heavenly shore;
      Therefore we sigh
    For those bright worlds on high,
Where reigns the Lord our God in majesty;
      There shall our joy
    Be pure from all alloy.

WHITSUNTIDE.

"His arrow shall go forth as the lightning."

When on the holy Jesus fell
    The Spirit, like a dove,
God by that sign designed to tell
    A mystery of love;
Confined to Israel's narrow bound
As yet the glorious Gospel-sound,
Where *gently* Jesus with his word
The spirit of his people stirred:

But when upon the faithful came,
    In God's appointed hour,
With rushing wind and cloven flame,
    The Spirit in his power,
Sign, *then* had come the promised day,
The Word should speed resistless way,
From pole to pole, from sea to sea,
With shout, and song, and victory.

Lord, let the lightning of thy word,
　　The thunder of thy power
In every clime be seen and heard,
　　Till all mankind adore,
Till all are gentle as the dove,
And all are fired with holy love,
And all resound with glad acclaim
The wonders of the threefold Name.

DULL EARS, HARD HEARTS.

"He causeth the wind to blow, and the waters flow."

Blow, wind; beat, rain;
Come, thou swift hurricane,
And echo forth thy voice to sinful men;
Stun their dull ears,
Wake up their dormant fears,
And make them think of past and coming years.

Th' Almighty's breath
Through the world's length and breadth
Carried the tidings forth of life and death;
Calm as the dove
Descending from above
The Spirit whispered words of heavenly love.

THE SPIRIT AND THE MUSE.

Man in his pride
God's truth has quite defied,
Himself his counsellor, his trust, his guide;
The pedant's lore,
Earth's yellow glittering ore—
These are the idols that he falls before!

Blow, wind; beat, rain;
Come, thou swift hurricane,
And echo forth thy voice to sinful men;
Stun their dull ears,
Wake up their dormant fears,
And make them think of past and coming years.

JESUS THE LIGHT OF THE WORLD.

"He that followeth me shall not walk in darkness, but shall have the light of life."

When in the wilderness,
Faint and provisionless,
Israel was wandering,
God's overshadowing
Fiery presence in glory was seen.

Christ, like a beacon-light,
Shines through the dark of night,
Leading the saints of God
By the way *he* has trod,
Till they reach safely in heaven their abode.

Christian wayfaring men,
Take up your crosses, then;
Jesus both can and will
Guide and support us, till
We too come safely to Zion's fair hill :

There shall all labours cease,
There shall be joy and peace,
There every living thing
Shall without ceasing sing
Praises to Jesus, our God and our King.

STILLING THE TEMPEST.

. "The wind and the sea obey him."

The wind, it came down with a gusty sweep
 From Galilee's hills on the peaceful deep,
Which was lifted on high by the tempest's breath,
 And threatened beneath with the chasms of death.

The hearts of the sailors were valiant and true,
 But fiercer and fiercer the wild wind blew,
And the billowy surge swept over the deck,
 And the ship was covered, and all but a wreck.

There was but One who had power to save
 The poor stricken souls from a watery grave,
But He lay, in spite of the storm on the deep,
 Behind on a pillow, and fast asleep.

The disciples made haste the Lord to awake,
  To behold the tempest that shook the lake;
"And carest thou not, good Master"—they said—
  "O save us, we perish without thy aid."

Then the Lord arose, and rebuked the deep,
  And commanded the winds to be hushed in sleep,
And the winds and the waves that instant cease,
  And all is again in perfect peace.

'Tis thus, as we sail o'er the waters of life,
  We are tost on a sea of tempestuous strife,
But the flood shall not drown us, our Guardian is he
  Who can still with a word the wind and the sea.

THE GODLY MAN.

" The world passeth away and the lust thereof, but he that doeth the will of God abideth for ever."

Shifted by every wind that blows,
Nor rest nor peace the worldling knows.
Unsafe his path, unfixed his aim,
His highest hope an earthly fame.

The man of God holds straight his course,
Unshaken by the tempest's force,
His trust is in the Lord most high,
His hope a mansion in the sky.

Lord, give me grace with all my heart
To choose and love the better part,
That, when this world shall cease to be,
I may in Heaven thy glory see.

REPENTANCE FROM DEAD WORKS.

" Prepare to meet thy God."

O sinner, thou the path of life hast trod,
    But not with God!
Soon will a few short years have passed away,
    Say, sinner, say,
What *then* the world to thee with all its show?
    Nothing, I trow:
Dar'st thou then meet in yon dark world alone
    The Holy One?
Dar'st thou then stand before him, calm and brave,
    Child of the grave?
Will not the very thought that *He* is near
    Thrill thee with fear?
When he shall call thee to account at last
    For sins long past,
What wilt thou say to him, or how withstand
    His mighty hand?
Turn—for thy God is merciful and just—
    Or die thou must.

CONFESSION OF SIN.

"If we confess our sins, he is faithful and just to forgive us our sins."

Those evil humours which oft lurk within
These mortal frames of ours, the fruits of sin,
Better discharge through sundry fleshly pores,
Red pimples, ugly blisters, ulcered sores,
Than let them unimpeded run their course,
And by degrees poison life's very source :
Just the same law effectual will be found
To make the spirit as the body sound ;
The act of sin, which baffled every eye,
Save His, who seeth all iniquity,
If closely harboured in the sinner's breast,
And unrepented of and unconfest,
Will poison with its taint each vital part,
And at the last defy all healing art.

Therefore the great Physician with the knife
Would probe the wound, to save the precious life:
Thou, who art conscious of some sinful sore
Eating unseen into thine inmost core,
Go, seek the Healer, ask him to impart
Health to thy soul, and tell him all thy heart;
For better far confess the sin, than wait
Until the sickness spreads, and it's too late.

THE TALE OF OUR SINS.

" Who can tell how oft he offendeth ?"

As many as the stars which in the heavens are seen;
As many as the flowers, strown gaily o'er the green;
As many as the drops, descending in the shower;
As many as the leaves, which fall in Autumn's hour;
As many as the sands, which lie upon the shore,
So many are the sins, alas! which we deplore;
    Our only hope is in the blood
    Of Jesus Christ, our Lord and God.

CHRISTIAN WISDOM.

" Christ the wisdom of God."

The highest wisdom which this world can give
Can never teach us how we ought to live,
And yet, if this we know not, all we know
Doth but increase our heritage of woe.

If we would seek true wisdom to attain,
We first must know that Christ alone is gain;
The countless treasures of the heavens and earth,
Lacking this treasure, are as nothing worth.

Long may we search with travail and with pain,
And think, because we find not, search is vain,
Yet must we not despair, but persevere—
Oft, when we think him furthest, Christ is near.

Leave we to him to fix the time and place,
The measure and the manner of his grace,
In all his dispensations let us rest,
Of one thing sure, that *He* knows what is best.

PRAYER.

"Pray without ceasing."

Cast, O my soul, aside
Thy sorrow and thy fear;
No matter what betide,
Do thou to God draw near.

Draw near unto the throne,
The Father's throne on high,
Where sits the only Son
In gracious majesty.

The Lord is still the same,
Thy heart and voice prepare;
In his most holy Name
Draw near, my soul, in prayer.

Thou shalt not pray in vain,
If thus thou wilt draw near;
Have faith in Him, and then
Thy way shall be made clear.

But, ere thou dost implore
Fresh blessings from above,
Forget not to adore
Aad thank him for his love;

For all that he has done,
For all that he has given,
But chiefly for his Son,
His precious gift from heaven.

And count it not a task
Thus ever to draw near;
If they would have who ask,
They needs must persevere.

In sickness and in health,
In sorrow, joy, or fear,
In times of want, in wealth,
Still stedfastly draw near.

So in the solemn hour,
When prayer itself must cease,
When He, whose word is power,
Shall will the soul's release,

Though weeping they shall bear
The dead corpse to its place,
The soul, borne through the air,
Shall see God face to face.

THE IMPERFECTION OF OUR PRAYERS.

" We know not how to pray as we ought."

O God, we are so weak,
That, even when we seek
   Thy face in prayer,
We know not what to say,
We know not how to pray,
   Nor when, nor where.

Fulfil, then, gracious Lord,
For us thy promised word,
   That, wheresoe'er
But two or three shall meet
In thy communion sweet,
   Thou wilt be there.

THE BLESSED OF THE LORD.

"Come unto me, all ye that are heavy laden, and I will give you rest."

  It was not those who pressed
And jostled round the Lord, who loved him best;
  Not those who in the crowd
Were heard to sound his praise with voices loud;
  Many were halt and blind,
Many, though sound in limb, were sick in mind;
  Some shrank in holy fear,
And some in silent sorrow shed the tear:
  Think you, they were unblest?
  O no! He gave them rest.

Zacchæus ran before,
And climbed to see him up a sycomore,
　　Nor guessed the Saviour's eye
Would notice, as mid thousands He passed by;
　　And one there was who knew
That Jesus by a word his works could do,
　　And would not have him come
Within a Gentile soldier's humble-home:
　　These were the men who heard
　　Salvation's gracious word.

It was the Saviour's boast
That he had come to seek and save the lost,
　　And oh! most tenderly
He showed to all his love and sympathy,
　　Nor was it only *then*
That Jesus ministered to sinful men:
　　Still does his watchful eye
Take note of every tear, of every sigh:
　　So kiud and yet so just
　　Is He in whom we trust.

THE BLOOD OF THE ATONEMENT.

"The blood of Jesus that speaketh better things than that of Abel."

When Cain had spilt his brother's blood,
   Earth, which drank up the purple flood,
Cried to the God of heaven to ban
   With awful curse that wicked man.

The blood of Jesus, who was slain
   By his own brethren, worse than Cain,
Pleads with the Father to forgive,
   And let the guilty sinners live.

O precious stream! mysterious blood
   Which from the side of Jesus flowed!
Balm of the soul! sure pledge and sign
   Thou, Lord, art ours, and we are thine.

THE BLESSEDNESS OF POVERTY.

" The love of money is the root of all evil."

Who would not rather for his lot
Have the poor peasant's humble cot,
Where, though his fare were scant and rude,
His days were spent in doing good,
Than yon large house for his abode
Far from the love and peace of God,
Though every dainty decked the board,
Which earth and air and sea afford ?
Too often riches spoil the heart,
And make the man from God depart ;
While gloating o'er the golden store,
And ever wishing it were more,
The eye is dimmed, and cannot see
The glories of eternity.
What shameful deeds have not been done,

Prompted by gold, beneath the sun!
What falsehoods told! what forgeries!
What frauds! what foul conspiracies!
Thefts, murders, rapines, wars, and blood
Flowing in one continuons flood;
The bands of friendship cut in twain—
Prayers and entreaties all were vain—
The strong exulting in their might,
The weak man crushed, robbed of his right;
These left to pine with scarce a crust,
Those squandering gold as if 'twere dust:
No man can tell the countless crimes
Which gold has caused thousands of times.
Therefore it was that Jesus taught
That this world's riches were but naught;'
He came not in great pomp and state,
He *chose* the poor man's low estate,
To them first preached his blessèd word,
For them pronounced the great reward,
From them he took his faithful few,
Leagued with himself his work to do:
Who *now* the rich would idolize?
Or who the poor man dare despise?
Such men have never Jesus known,

Jesus will never such men own;
Though in this world they pass for great,
Because they have a fine estate,
Because they happen to inherit
' Prizes of fortune, not of merit,'
Yet all so soon as they by fate
Have finished with this mortal state,
They're destitute and desolate,
Their abject spirits left to pine
Without one ray on them to shine,
While the poor souls, whom they were wont
To hold in very mean account,
Because they made it their chief pleasure
To seek the true and heavenly treasure,
No longer in their sorry plight,
Shine forth, like stars in dark of night.
Then seek not to be rich, my friend,
For this world's riches have an end,
And they, who in them put their trust,
Will find they've gotten nought but dust;
Lift up thine heart, lift up thine eyes,
Seek in the Heavens a lasting prize.

ILL-GOTTEN WEALTH.

"Woe to him that increaseth that which is not his! how long? and to him that ladeth himself with thick clay."

What hast thou here?
A goodly house and fair,
Wherein thou fondly thinkest to remain,
And reap the fruit of thine ill-gotten gain;
Have done:
Know'st thou not yet
Thy sun is almost set,
Thy mansion is the portal of the tomb;
And thou must enter soon the dark and dreadful gloom,

Thou hast great store
Of gold and silver ore,
But not one grain of it thou'lt take away,
Soon as thy soul doth quit its mortal clay;
Hast thought
That all thy state
Is nought
Which seems so great,
If in the land, where flits the parted ghost,
Houses, possessions, gold, nay, *thou thyself* art lost?

Make haste, thou fool,
Bring hither line and rule,
Build thee a habitation on the Rock,
Which shall endure the great and final shock,
When all
Of earth that's wrought
Must fall
And come to nought;
There fix thy dwelling, *there* lay up great store
Of that good treasure which doth last for evermore.

ALMSGIVING.

" Blessed are the merciful, for they shall obtain mercy."

Think we, *that* man shall lose his meed
Who helps the Christian in his need,
Who for the love of Jesus shows
Compassion to the poor man's woes;
Gives gladly of his little store,
And only wishes it were more,
Nor waits until one comes to ask,
As though it were some irksome task,
But, with quick eye to see the need,
As quickly does the generous deed;
Denies himself from day to day
To scatter blessings on his way,
Nor wearies in the work of love,
But trusts in Him who sees above—
His fragrance like sweet-smelling flowers
After the spring's refreshing showers—

Or, like the precious ointment shed
Profusely on the Saviour's head,
His perfume shall mount up on high,
And with sweet odour fill the sky—
The mighty Lord himself hath said,
That man shall never beg his bread;
The Lord shall be his staff and stay,
The Lord shall guide him on his way,
The Lord shall give him rich increase,
The Lord shall give him life and peace,
Angels shall bear him to his rest,
His place shall be among the blest:
When Jesus comes to wake the just
From their long slumber in the dust,
To endless glory he shall rise,
And shine for ever in the skies.

DIVINE TREASURE.

"More to be desired than gold."

Like to some hidden mine,
Where stores of precious metal shine,
Lost in the earth
Till labour comes and gives them birth,
God's records old,
Teeming with wealth untold,
Escape the eye
Of common folk who heedless pass them by;
But they, who prudently explore,
And work for God's good ore,
A vast material find
Of golden treasure to enrich the mind,
Which got, their love for it waxeth so great,
That nothing can its force abate;
All other labour counts as nought,
Pleasures by them are never sought,
One joy alone—God's word to know,
For this they bend, for this they bow.

WAITING FOR OUR CHANGE.

" To die is gain."

The Lord, who made the worlds above,
    Made this fair world below,
And in it tokens of his love
    And power all things show;

And, were it not we also see
    Tokens of sin and death,
Here we might almost wish to be
    For ever drawing breath :

But, as with each succeeding year
    Sorrows and cares increase,
We pray not to continue here,
    But *die*, and be at peace.

Yet not so much this world, as *we*,
 Who need a change of state,
Nor *can* we quite restorèd be,
 Till we have passed Death's gate.

With bodies changed, with souls renewed,
 New creatures we shall rise,
With higher powers by grace endued,
 To live in Paradise.

HEAVENLY REST.

"There remaineth a rest for the people of God."

The Heavenly rest!
Who would not so be blest?
This world so fair!
What doth it yield but care?
And yet we fear
To think that death is near!
Death is no foe,
'Twas God ordained it so;
When Jesus died,
Jesus was glorified;
Death sets us free
From earthly misery;
When dead, we are
In God's protecting care;
Our friends may weep,
But we shall calmly sleep:

Hope is not dead,
When this short life has fled:
Hope still survives,
And more than ever thrives:
Earth is no tomb,
Earth is man's second womb;
We rise again,
When Jesus comes to reign;
They who are his
Shall have eternal bliss.
Would *we* be blest,
Seek we the Heavenly rest;
Gain here is loss,
Our highest gain the Cross;
Faith, hope, and love—
These fit men for above.
This life once o'er,
We rest for evermore.

LIFE IN THE WILDERNESS.

"The Spirit driveth him into the wilderness.

To some wild desert glen
Far from the haunts of men
   God bids us go;
   Then be it so,
   For weal or woe.

What though we have our home,
Where wild beasts love to roam;
   Angels are near
   To minister—
   We will not fear.

When compassed round with pain
We shall not call in vain;
   Our Saviour bore
   For us before
   All this and more.

When in His Name we cry,
God will look down from high;
    He has the power,
    He is a tower
    In danger's hour.

Led by His mighty hand,
We soon shall reach the land,
    Where trials cease,
    Where joys increase,
    And all is peace.

To Him then we will raise
Our voices in glad praise,
    The Father, Son,
    And Holy One,
    One God alone.

THE CHRISTIAN SOLDIER.

"A good soldier of Jesus Christ."

Oftimes has the Christian soldier
    Fronted death upon the field,
Taught by Jesus Christ his Saviour
    Not to falter nor to yield.

Strong the forces which assail him,
    Full of craft the foe's attack,
Still, confiding in his Captain,
    Never will he turn his back.

Though his flesh be faint and weary,
    Though his body stricken down,
Yet his spirit, still unconquered,
    Triumphs in the promised crown.

O what glories are reservèd
   For the Lamb's triumphant host,
Far exceeding all the sufferings
   That in this world they have cost!

Onward, then, brave Christian warriors,
   Still maintain the glorious fight,
Let the traitors and fainthearted
   Choose a base disastrous flight.

CHRISTIAN WATCHFULNESS.

" Watch ye."

If God doth give thee peace.
Live not, as one at ease,
    Idling away
    Life's precious day,
Use thy time well, prepare
For the return of war:

For in this earthly clime
All things are changed by time;
    Nothing so sure
    As to endure;
No man, not even the best,
Finds upon earth his rest.

Look! to the fruitful earth
Seasons recur of dearth,
 Grass, which was green,
 No more is seen;
Winds, which were hushed in sleep,
Over the wild waves sweep,

Thus too the days of peace,
God gives thee here, must cease;
 While thou hast rest,
 To arm 'tis best,
Lest haply unprepared
Thou find thyself ensnared.

THE CHRISTIAN PILGRIM'S PROGRESS.

" Speak unto the children of Israel, that they go forward."

Ah! wherefore will not men take heed
In this their day, their hour of need,
And, mindful of the judgment, save
Their souls through Jesus from the grave?
When Jesus comes, too late 'twill be
To seek to change their destiny.

All earthly joys shall then have fled,
All friends be numbered with the dead,
And none but they, who here below
Have drunk with Christ the cup of woe,
Shall then behold the blest abode,
Where dwell the saints in peace with God.

Then, Christian brothers, let us take
Fresh courage, and fresh efforts make;
Serve not the world in this its hour
Of pomp and pride and fancied power;
Through clouds and darkness lies our way
To regions of eternal day.

The Lord Jehovah calls us on,
Our Captain is the Holy One,
And, as with joy we march along,
Angels will cheer us with their song;
When at the Lamb's high throne we bow,
Glory shall crown the victor's brow.

THE COMFORT OF SUFFERINGS.

"As ye are partakers of the sufferings, so also of the consolation."

Repine not at sufferings—we need them to prove
The strength of our faith, and the warmth of our love;
By a merciful Father from heaven they are sent,
And often as loving corrections are meant.

Repine not at sufferings—they bid us prepare
Our hearts and our souls and our voices for prayer;
They call us away from the follies of earth,
And make us look up to the land of our birth.

Repine not at sufferings—the Lord from on high
Came down from His glory to suffer and die;
For the gain set before him He recked not the loss,
For the sins of the world He was nailed to the Cross.

Repine not at sufferings—the more they increase,
The more shall our knowledge of God's blessèd peace;
They last not for ever; God wills them to cease,
And then we give thanks for the gracious release.

Repine not at sufferings—through sufferings we know
How to feel for our brethren, when *they* are in woe;
The hard heart is softened, the haughty brought low,
And the love, which burnt feebly, recovers its glow.

Repine not at sufferings—as gold, when refined,
Comes forth from the furnace the best of its kind,
So all men are provèd; the base suffer loss,
The sterling endure, and are purged from all dross.

THE MOST HOLY PLACE.

"The true tabernacle which the Lord pitched, and not man."

Think not these earthly temples are
The only houses meet for prayer,
In every place the Lord doth hear
The true and faithful worshipper.

There is a mystic Heavenly shrine,
Where sits enthroned the Lord divine,
Thither be all thy prayers addrest,
There seek the true and perfect rest.

Though surpliced priests meet not thine eye,
The great High Priest is ever nigh,
Thy fellow-worshippers are they
Who everywhere the Lord obey.

Go mix thee with that Heavenly throng,
Who day and night their praise prolong,
Who some below, and some above,
Are all close knit in bonds of love.

THE LIVING AND THE DEAD.

"Weep ye not for the dead, neither bemoan him."

Mourn not the saints, whose souls have fled,
And joined the myriads of the dead;
They rest, they rest, from sorrow free,
From sin, and earthly misery;
They would not, if they could, again
Visit the haunts of mortal men;
They would not fight the fight anew,
Albeit faithful, valiant, true;
Enough for them once to have spent
Life upon earth—they died content;
Their bliss without us not complete,
They wait till all in Christ shall meet.

But would'st thou mourn, mourn their sad lot,
Who, reft of friends, by man forgot,
In silent sorrow and distress
Wear out a life of loneliness;
Yea, mourn for those, who in despite
Of the High God confound the right,
Slaves of the world for gold, for power,
Or to enjoy the passing hour;
Mourn for *thyself*, if thou canst wear
Gaily a crown of rosebuds here;
If from thy soul the life has fled,
Breathe, breathe thou may'st, but thou art dead.

114 THE SPIRIT AND THE MUSE.

THE TREES OF EDEN.

"The tree of life in the midst of the garden, and the tree of knowledge of good and evil."

When God of old did place in Eden fair
The first-created happy human pair,
Two trees of divers fruits he there did plant,
And made in them a holy covenant;
The one forbidden—whoso ate, should know
Both good and evil, heritage of woe;
Not so the other—living fruit it bore,
That man might eat, and live for evermore:
Eve listened to the Tempter's subtle voice,
Put forth her hand and made the deadly choice;
Next gave to Adam; Adam not afraid,
Though *conscious* of the trespass, disobeyed.

Farewell the beauty of that garden fair!
Farewell the life so free from toil and care!
Ashamed and weeping, our first parents went
From Eden to their place of banishment;
And now the tree, the garden, are no more,
But sin and death, alas! we still deplore,

THE FALLEN TREE.

"Delivered unto death."

Tree that hast weathered many a blast,
Uprooted by the storm at last,
No more shalt thou, with graceful ease,
Bend to each fitful passing breeze;
No more, at Spring's return, be seen
Rich in thy dress of gladsome green;
No more afford a grateful shade
To those who saunter o'er the glade;
The ruthless storm has laid thee low,
The axe shall lop thee bough by bough,
The fire shall burn thy strength and pride,
Which storm and axe and fire defied;
What made thee thus an easy prey?
Was it thine age? or did decay?
Or has the worm scooped him a bed
Within thy trunk, and on thee fed?

Whate'er the cause, cruel the blow.
Which laid thee prematurely low,
While all around thy compeers tower,
Defiant of the Tempest's power.
  But wherefore muse upon thy state?
Such is my own, such others' fate:
A thousand chances ready stand
To execute the Lord's command;
The worm, the sword, a passing breath—
All are the ministers of death;
Unseen the hand which deals the blow,
The blow is dealt—'tis all we know:
To day in life, in health, in bloom—
To-morrow tenants of the tomb!
Nor age alone is doomed to fall,
Death strikes with cruel axe at *all*:
Scarce has the infant sucked the breast,
'Tis called for ever to its rest;
The tender child, like some fair flower,
Droops, sickens, dies, in one short hour;
Youth with its hope, man in his prime,
There's none who lives but has his time:
Not all the treasured stores of earth,
Not beauty, wisdom, rank, or worth,

Can interpose a brief delay,
Or purchase man one other day;
Or rich or poor, or high or low,
None can escape the fatal blow.
  Yet not as trees we fall and die,
Ours is a higher destiny;
The Lord, to save us from the doom,
Himself lay lifeless in the tomb,
Suffered no ravage from decay,
Till thrice the sun brought round the day,
Then with the golden morn came forth,
Bursting the prison-gates of earth,
Displayed the trophies of his power
In the new life his body bore,
And in the fulness of his might,
His chosen wondering at the sight,
Uplifted to the heaven, withdrew
Hid by a cloud from mortal view.
Where now, O Death, thy vaunted sting?
Where are thy terrors, mighty King?
Hell and the grave are now no more,
The Lord from Heaven—He has the power:
Our God shall come, and at his voice
Earth shall be glad and Heaven rejoice,

The mouldering fragments of the tomb
Fresh life and beauty shall assume,
And rise in glory to adore
The triumphs of his Love and Power.

CULTURE OF THE SOUL.

"Break up thy fallow land."

The sin so small
We scarce can think it is a sin at all
　Will, if let go,
Become at last a mighty world of woe,
　Just as the seed,
Chance-dropt at times, of some pernicious weed,
　Left in the ground,
Will strangle all fair flowers which grow around :
　Therefore beware,
And exercise betimes a watchful care ;
　Grudge not the toil,
Search well thy heart, and throughly cleanse the soil ;
　Each lusty vice
Cut off at once at any sacrifice ;

The vacant room
Fill with choice plants of everlasting bloom;
　　Ask God to bless
And make more fruitful still thy fruitfulness;
　　So shalt thou be
Meet to be called the Lord God's husbandry;
　　For *His* thou art,
He owns by right the acres of thy heart,
　　And He has given
Whatever flower or fruit in thee has thriven.

THE RIVER OF LIFE.

" He showed me a pure river of water of life, clear as crystal."

Fountain of life, whose stricken side
Gives forth a pure and heavenly tide,
Whose living waters' ceaseless flow
Gladdens this wilderness below;

As weary on the world's highway
I journey on from day to day,
I love to rest by thee awhile,
And find refreshment from my toil;

I love to stand alone, and gaze,
As up and down the bright flood plays,
And with the music of the stream
To lose myself in holy dream:

Here on thy pure and hallowed brink
Methinks that Angels pause to drink,
And, as the waters rise and fall,
I seem to hear the Spirit's call;

In yonder wave, which shines so bright,
Hope glistens with immortal light,
And in those crystal depths I see
A mirror of God's purity.

Thus musing I forget my care,
And soar away to regions, where
The saints of God, a countless band,
Before the throne in glory stand:

There, issuing from the golden mount,
Which hides its deep unfathomed fount,
A River, clear as crystal, laves
The Heavenly shores with living waves.

THE SOUTHERN CROSS.

" Looking unto Jesus."

'Tis said that in the Southern sky
The traveller, when night is nigh,
Sees in the vault of heaven a sign,
A starry Cross, conspicuous shine,
Which guides and cheers him on his way,
Till breaks the dawn of coming day.

'Tis thus the Christian pilgrims see,
Lighting this dark world gloriously,
The Cross of Jesus—as they roam,
Pointing to their eternal home :
They take fresh courage at the view,
And joyfully their way pursue.

No harm the Christian can betide,
Who takes the Cross to be his guide;
It gilds the portals of the tomb,
It lights him through the nether gloom,
Till he beholds in brighter skies
The world's great Sun in glory rise.

THE LILIES.

"Consider the lilies of the field."

Lilies with your golden hue
Glistening in the morning dew,
Who more richly robed than you?
Kings cannot, with all their state,
Your fair glory emulate.

Lilies, you shall die and rot,
And your beauty be forgot,
One short day and you are not:
We, who are but common clay,
Shall outshine your bright array.

For the same Creative Power,
Who has bid you live and flower,
Who has fed you with His shower,
Has a fairer world than this
For the choice ones that are His.

In a land of golden light,
Clad in robes of Heavenly white,
Ever living, ever bright,
They their voices high upraise
To exalt their Maker's praise.

RAIN FROM HEAVEN.

" Thy clouds drop fatness."

Ye clouds of rain,
Come round again
To swell the grain
And make the earth
Hasten its birth,
Wetting the clod
With dew of God—
To make this isle
With verdure smile,
And all its bowers
Alive with flowers —
Treasures untold
Of purest gold
Not half so precious are,
As the rich drops of moisture ye in heaven do bear.

And yet than you
More rich that dew,
Which from the throne
Of God comes down,
Causing to live,
Causing to thrive
Regions accurst,
Dying of thirst,
Men's hearts, within
Blasted with sin;
There fruits are found,
There flowers abound,
Life's fruits and flowers which glow
Where the quick streams of Paradise for ever flow.

LIVING WATERS.

St. Govor's Fountain, Kensington Gardens.

Not St. Govor, but the Lord
Doth this well-spring, man, afford;
Ere thou take the cup to drink,
Pause, and of the Giver think;
God, who bade the water flow,
Keeps it ever running so;
If it seem to thee but small,
'Tis enough for thee—for *all*:
All may come and quench their thirst,
Fares the last, as fares the first:
Winter, summer, morn, or eve,
Never will this spring deceive,
From such mighty depths below
Doth it without ceasing flow:
Here's a draught, both fresh and clear,
For the beggar, for the peer;

Money is not here required,
Thankfulness alone's desired;
Nor for *that* its worth abate,
Not one drop couldst thou create:
What would all thy gold avail,
If God bade the water fail?
He alone can give, and He
Gives it without stint to thee:
Take His gift, then, nor forget
There are better waters yet,
Precious, priceless, freely given,
Not of earth, sent down from Heaven,
Living waters which make whole
And refresh the thirsting soul:
Jesus is their Fountain-head,
Drink—or else thy soul is dead.

THE FATHERLAND.

"We, according to his promise, look for new heavens and a new earth."

What is the Fatherland?
'Tis not the land, as the Germans feign,
Where the Germans live, where the Germans reign;
'Tis not the land, which was held by our sires,
With its peaceful homes and its hallowed spires;
'Tis not the poor little parcel of earth,
Which a man can name as the spot of his birth;
'Tis not the broadest inhabited space,
Which is owned, or is claimed, by a single race;
The Ocean does not encompass it round
With its foaming waves and its roaring sound;
They, who would give us a Fatherland so,
Give us a land but of change and of woe :
Whoso would know what the Fatherland *is*,
Must look in God's book at the Promises;

That is the land, which in vision was shown,
Which to Abr'am and Isaac and Jacob was known,
A land, with milk and honey which flows,
A land, which no sin nor sorrow knows,
Which only by faith can be here possest,
Where the good men departed do find a rest,
Where a countless band of the Heavenly host
Sing the Father, the Son, and the Holy Ghost,
A land of joy and a land of love,
A true Fatherland in the Heavens above.

THE TEMPLE OF THE LORD.

"Thus saith the High and lofty One, that inhabiteth eternity, whose Name is Holy, I dwell in the high and holy place, with him also that is of a humble and contrite spirit, to revive the spirit of the humble, and to revive the heart of the contrite ones."

While wandering on my path alone,
Musing of men and ages gone,
The Spirit led me to survey
The monuments which crossed my way,
The tribute of a nation's praise
To mighty men of bygone days:
Patriot and conqueror were there,
The statesman and philosopher,
Poet, and orator whose word
Thousands in breathless silence heard,
Kings, princes, chiefs, now only known
By column, statue, bronze, or stone.

Thus was I musing on my way,
Methought I heard the Spirit say :
" Not many of the men you see
" Were worthy of this dignity :
" Some, leading forth an armèd host,
" In slaught'ring thousands made their boast;
" Some by a lying eloquence
" Obtained a bad pre-eminence ;
" Some wrang their riches from the poor,
" And turned the widow from their door ;
" They coveted an earthly fame,
" And on the earth they *have* a name ;
" They left stern duty's narrow path,
" And made a covenant with death ;
" Their highest aim the world to please,
" They gat its honours, riches, ease :
" What monument have you passed by
" Of Jesus Christ, your Lord on high,
" Who heard Creation's heavy sigh,
" And stooped from mansions in the sky,
" Submitted to become a slave
" And for the world his life-blood gave,
" Nailed to the Cross the sin and curse,
" Gave freedom to the Universe ? "

I looked, if haply I might see
Something to his dear memory;
I saw the vast Cathedral dome,
The centre of our mighty Rome;
I heard the old grey Abbey tower
Sound forth the solemn passing hour;
A hundred steeples met my eyes,
Pointing to Jesus in the skies—
Memorials surely these, I said,
Of him who lives, who once was dead.
" And do you think," the Angel cried,
" These spectacles of human pride
" Can aught avail to celebrate
" The virtues of the good and great?
" Though glorious to the eye of man,
" Whose life's a breath, his days a span,
" These are no more than common clay,
" Destined themselves to pass away;
" Each fleeting year, each month, each day
" But marks the progress of decay:
" Doubt not, of old great deeds were done
" Great battles fought, great vict'ries won,
" In ev'ry age they've sought to raise
" A lasting monument of praise;

"They've hewn the marble from the rock,
"Giv'n shape and beauty to the block,
"Pourtrayed on canvas to the life
"The scene of bloodshed and of strife,
"Reared palace, castle, city, tower,
"The fancied triumphs of their power;
"Where are they now?—A few remain
"To chronicle that all is vain;
"The most have vanished from their place,
"There's not a remnant, not a trace:
"Where once exulting millions trod,
"The green grass grows upon the sod;
"Where flourished cities great and fair,
"There now the wild beast makes his lair;
"And these, too, which you now behold,
"Hoary with age, o'ergrown with mould,
"Swept by the shock of Time's rude hand,
"Shall lie like wrecks upon the strand,
"And haply some one passing by
"In days to come shall heave a sigh,
"And cry, 'Alas the vanity!'
"If outward object could proclaim
"The greatness of the Saviour's name,
"No need of human skill or power,

"Nor stately dome, nor massive tower,
"Nor statuary's plastic art,
"Nor painting's vivid counterpart,
"Nor gold, nor precious stones, nor brass,
"Nor carvèd oak, nor stainèd glass:
"Behold the heavens spread out on high,
"The earth with all its majesty,
"The mountains standing in their pride,
"The mighty ocean's restless tide,
"The sun and moon's unfailing light
"To rule the day and rule the night—
"This were a fitting Temple, where
"The whole Creation joins in prayer;
"This were a worthy monument
"Of Him who is omnipotent.
"But would you know the hallowed cell
"Wherein the Saviour loves to dwell?
"Go seek the man of lowly life,
"Who keeps his tongue from guile and strife,
"Harbours no malice in his heart,
"Cleaves close unto the better part,
"Pure as the Angels are above,
"Strong in the power of faith and love,
"Walking in pleasant paths of peace,

" Looking for death as his release,
" No stately structure of decay,
" No cold fair form of lifeless clay,
" A living Temple, holy shrine,
" The image of the Lord divine,
" This is the man, yes, this is he
" Who keeps alive Christ's memory."

GOOD FRUITS.

"Their works do follow them."

Naked as when we left our mother's womb
We're carried to our tomb,
Yet not for *that* is life of little gain;
    Our holy deeds remain :
    For as in Autumn-time,
    When fruits are in their prime,
An agèd tree, set in an orchard fair,
Can scarce unpropped its load of fruitage bear,
Then comes a storm, and, smitten by the blast,
It holds no longer but succumbs at last,
Yet even in its fall it has not lost
The mighty load of fruit which is its boast;
    So we must bow the head,
    And join the countless dead,
    Yet good men are not left,
    Even when dead, bereft ;
They bear with them below a glorious load
Of good fruit as an off'ring to their God.

LIFE FROM THE DEAD.

"The shadow of heavenly things."

These outward things—how much they show
Of things above to men below!
They live, they die, they rise again—
Lesson of hope to mortal men:

Planted in this God's earthly bower,
We blossom just one little hour,
Our blossom fades, we droop, we die,
And in the earth awhile we lie,

Till, in the world's great Springtide, we
Shall by God's Spirit quickened be,
And richer fruits and flowers display
In brighter climes an endless day.

SEED - TIME AND HARVEST.

"Look down from thy holy habitation, and bless thy people Israel."

Unfruitful though I be,
And barren, Lord, to thee,
Yet do thou come to me,
And sow my heart again
With thy most holy grain,
And make it take deep root,
And live and upward shoot,
That, when thy Angels come
To take the Harvest home,
A large and goodly yield
Be found in me, thy field,
And precious golden store
From me be gathered in to Heaven's great garner floor,
For which to Thee will be the praise and glory, Lord, for evermore.

THE TARES.

"Whence hath it tares?"

Thou wicked weed,
Who dropped thy seed
Into the earth
To cause a dearth,
Aping so vain
The goodly grain?
Some damnèd wight,
The child of Night
Or goblin foul,
Or loathsome fowl,
Or hell-born breath
Laden with death:
Thou shalt not stay
To mock the day,
Thou shalt not curse
The ground thy nurse,
Thou shalt not spoil
The reaper's toil;

This hand shall tear
And lay thee bare,
So that thy root
No more shall shoot;
There thou shalt lie;
And there shalt *die*,
The sun's hot flame
Shall burn thy shame,
Storms with their lash
Shall drive thine ash:
This is thy meed,
Thou wicked weed.

THE TREES OF THE WOOD.

"That which is crooked cannot be made straight."

As, walking through a wood, one sees
Some straight, and other crookèd trees,
And even those, which straightest grow,
Are not quite faultless every bough,
While e'en the crookedest we see
Yet have a naked dignity;
So in the world—some men are good;
These are the straight ones of the wood;
Others are badly natured; these,
Just like those crookèd ones, displease:
Yet take the best, you will not find
That they are perfect of their kind;
Or take the worst, and they excel
In parts the ones you like right well;

Thus Nature tells us to beware,
And both our praise and censure spare;
For not a soul beneath Heaven's vault
But hath or here or there a fault,
Nor one so monstrously misgrown
But hath some beauty for its own.

THE LEAVES OF THE WOOD.

" As of the green leaves on a thick tree, so is the generation of flesh and blood."

Bright green, and then a darker hue,
But still most rich the foliage is to view;
Then darker still, but just
A little marrèd with the sun and dust;
Ere long the forest is one mass of gold,
Which tells us that the leaves are getting old;
Then let the north wind blow, or only just
A little breeze, or sharp and sudden gust,
Soon all the glory of the wood is seen
Scattered, or piled in heaps upon the green;
The trees have lost their crown,
The dead damp leaves are turned to earthy brown
And with the winter's gloom
They're sunk in Earth's deep tomb :
Thus all created things do pass away,
And Man too hás his day ;
Childhood, youth, manhood, age—when these are gone,
His cycle is complete, his year is done.

THE SAVIOUR AND THE SINNER.

"Blotting out the handwriting."

THE VOICE OF THE SAVIOUR:

"Spend life away,
Trifle and play,
But know that there shall surely be a day,
When God shall bring
To judgment every work with every secret thing."

THE VOICE OF THE SINNER:

"O Lord, I fall
Confessing all
The sins which I have done, both great and small;
My debts forgive,
And in the greatness of Thy mercy let me live."

THE VOICE OF THE SAVIOUR:

"Thy debts are paid,
Thy peace is made,
Only no longer dwell amongst the dead;
Begin anew
And let thy life henceforth be holy, just, and true.''

THE VOICE OF THE SINNER:

"Lord, I will raise
The voice of praise
To Thee for all the remnant of my days;
Thou hast made whole,
Meet that I should to Thee devote my thankful soul.'

A SACRIFICE FOR SIN.

" Christ died for our sins."

How full of comfort is this word,
That Jesus died, our God and Lord!
Died for our sins! amazing thought!
For us poor creatures, sons of nought!

Now, though like Jesus die we must,
We shall not perish in the dust;
Like Jesus, we shall rise again;
Like Jesus, live; like Jesus, reign.

Then let us, while on earth we stay,
Quit us like children of the day,
Live to our God, by all be known
As heirs of Heaven, as Jesus' own.

CRUELTY TO ANIMALS.

" The beasts of the field cry also unto thee."

When God ordained that men
Should over all the brute creation reign,
    He did not will that they
Should hold a merciless and cruel sway,
      But the poor beasts should spare,
And treat them with a kind and generous care,
      And with a gentle hand
Accustom them to work at their command—
    Either to draw the plough,
Or carry burthens with sure foot and slow;
    Or gallop o'er the plain,
Or listen to the driver's guiding rein;
      Some to give wholesome food,
Others to yield men clothing, warm and good;

To fill the world around
With beauty, life, and motion, and sweet sound,
And by their wondrous frame
To tell abroad their great Creator's name :
Such was the Heavenly plan,
Man for the beast was made, and beast for man.
Fie on our fallen race,
Which hath perverted quite God's law of grace!
To Heaven the cattle cry ;
Will not the Lord avenge them from on high ?
Look how the horses strain!
The brutal driver flogs them might and main!
Look at those beasts uncouth,
Footsore and weary, foaming at the mouth!
See how those way-worn sheep
Limp as they go! It almost makes one weep.
Rarer and yet more rare
The notes and plumage of the song-birds are ;
For with such wanton fun
They're slain by scores with net and trap and gun !
Therefore sad plagues are rife,
The fly and worm eat up the corn of life ;
Beasts perish in the field,
The Earth withholds the fatness of her yield ;

Lean Want and Sickness pale,
And ghastly Death come on, scourges of Hell,
And Discord waves her brand,
Ready to kindle flames thro' all the land:
Not undeserved the rod,
Wilful we sin 'gainst beast, and man, and God.

THE GOOD SHEPHERD.

"Behold, I, even I, will both search my sheep, and seek them out:
. . . . . I will feed them in a good pasture, and upon the
high mountains of Israel shall their food be."

When Jesus came and dwelt on earth of old,
He was the Shepherd, Israel was the fold,
No ravening wolves approached the flock he kept,
They lay in safety, and in safety slept,
He led them forth where the green pastures grow,
Led them to brooks where living waters flow,
And, when the Smiter came, the sheep to save
His own most precious life the Shepherd gave.

Soon from the dead by God's Almighty power,
The smitten Shepherd rose to die no more;
The scattered sheep he gathered once again,
And took away their sorrow and their pain;
Gave, ere he left them, pastors of his choice,
And bade them follow and obey their voice,
Till he should fetch them to the Heavenly shore,
In whose bright pastures they should want no more.

All ye who seek the Saviour's love to share,
Show to the Saviour's flock a shepherd's care,
Feed ye the hungry, give the thirsty drink,
Rescue the falling from the dangerous brink,
Bind up the broken, seek the lost and stray,
Be watchful lest the sheep become a prey,
For, when of old one sought his love to show,
The Saviour bade him *feed His flock below.*

THE FISHERS.

"From henceforth thou shalt catch men."

Upon old Galilee's shore,
Their toil of fishing o'er,
Two brothers, leaving all,
Followed the Master's call,
No longer now to take,
Fish from their native lake,
But on a stormier sea,
Fishers of *men* to be.
Ye faithful ones, who sweep
The World's tempestuous deep,
Plying your holy craft,
Mankind your precious draught,
While lasts the timely Night,
Ere breaks the Morning light,

Watch for the favouring tide
To scour the waters wide.
See, every creek and bay
Teems with the living prey,
The wandering myriads wait
The fisher's gathering net:
Launch out into the deep,
Throughly the waters sweep,
Heed not the ocean's roar,
But haul the net ashore.

THE PROMISE OF THE FATHER.

"The Holy Ghost fell on them."

A preacher to the people spake,
How Jesus died for sinners' sake,
    How Jesus rose,
    And pardoned those
Who leagued them with his mortal foes :
    They heard, they heard,
    They were *not* stirred
    By the great word.

Till, coming from the Heavens above,
The Holy Ghost, God's gift of love,
    Opened their ears,
    Aroused their fears,
Showed them God's love, and drew their tears :
    Then, when they heard,
    Much were they stirred
    By the great word.

SPIRITUAL UTTERANCES.

"Combining spiritual things with spiritual."

The weapons of the warfare of the Lord
Are not the gun, the javelin, the sword,
No, nor the words which men of deepest thought
Have in the schools with much brain-labour wrought,
But the fresh speakings, set by fools at nought,
God by his Spirit hath to good men taught,
Quick as the lightning, strong as any fire,
Searching heart secrets, inflaming desire,
Refreshing as the dew upon the grass,
Reflecting Heavenly things clearly as glass,

---

* Such, I am confident, is the only proper rendering of πνευματικοῖς πνευματικὰ συγκρίνοντες, in I. Cor. ii. 13. Understand λόγοις. It was a question not of *comparison* but of *combination*. 'What were the best *words* in which to preach the things of God'? The Apostle answers, "Not in the words which man's wisdom teacheth, but which the Holy Ghost teacheth." The *things* were πνευματικά, the *words* should be πνευματικοί also. It is to be hoped that the Revisionists will set this passage right.

Simple yet striking, gracious, winning, wise ;
Such words belike they speak in Paradise,
'Tis not enough the way of truth to know,
If we would preach it, God must tell us how,
Lest peradventure, while we would combine
Words of man's wisdom with the things divine,
Truth, ill discharged, be reft of half its force,
And, like an arrow, fall short in its course.

SIGNS OF THE TIMES.

"Behold the fig tree."

The Lord once said, that, when we see
The blossoming fig and budding tree,
We know at once the time of year,
We know that Summer then is near;
So in the world, when we descry,
By vision of our mental eye,
The various changes of this life,
Plague, famine; earthquake, battle, strife,
Though human agents speak the word,
And fleshly warriors wield the sword,
And all that happens seems to be
The chances of mortality,

Yet, if we view the scene aright,
And have not dimmed our inner sight,
These are but buds and leaves which show
That God is reigning here below;
Fresh burstings of His mighty power
Are visible in that strange hour,
And they who seek Him shall not fail
His glorious presence then to hail.

HOPE AMID BILLOWS.

*"The waves of the sea are mighty, and rage horribly,
But yet the Lord, who dwelleth on high, is mightier."*

Come, let us to the mountain flee,
Far from the wild tumultuous sea
Of nations rushing to and fro,
The saints of God to overthrow.

Standing upon th' eternal Rock,
We will not fear the tempest's shock,
But calmly wait until the tide
Of furious passions shall subside.

The Word of God has mightier force
Than Ocean rolling in his course,
Than thunder echoing through the sky,
Than the fierce whirlwind sweeping by.

When God commands the storm to cease,
Straightway the Ocean is at peace,
And favouring breezes waft us o'er
Calm waters to the Heavenly shore.

THE CARCASE - VULTURES.

"Wheresoever the carcase is, there will the eagles be gathered together."

As, when upon seas
Where sweeps the wild breeze,
A tempest-tost vessel scarce holds on her way,
And the mariners cry
To the great God on high,
For 'tis vain now to look to the sheltering bay,

The wreck-scene soon brings
On the hurricane's wings
The ravening sea-birds that wait for the prey,
And boldly they wheel,
And close to the keel,
Which scarce can be seen through the foam and the spray,

Or as when armed men
On field, hill, and glen,
Are massing by thousands to join in the fray;
Night covers them all
With her solemn black pall,
And in silence they wait for the dawn of the day;

Lo! ere the morn break,
There float in their wake
The vultures who love to the battle to flock;
They scent from afar
The banquet of war,
And wait for the carcase to fall by the shock:

'Twill be so in the hour,
When with wrath and great power
The Devil comes down to trouble the earth,
When the death-blasts of Hell
Shall rage and shall swell,
And many shall curse the day of their birth.

For Terror shall reign,
And Sorrow, and Pain,
And the Sword shall devour, and the Plague, and the Dearth,
And kingdoms shall shake,
And nations shall quake,
For fear of the judgments that come on the earth.

Ah! many a deck
Shall then be a wreck,
Which now moves so fair o'er the waters of life,
And many shall cry
To the great God on high,
Who now little reck of the storm and the strife.

And then shall arise,
Full of blasphemous lies,
False Christs and false prophets, intent upon prey;
They shall run to and fro,
They shall sing the loud woe,
And by great signs and wonders shall draw men away.

For these birds of the air
For themselves only care,
As they follow the havoc of Hell and of Death;
When the Heavens are clear,
Then they no where appear,
For they love not the calm of the Heavenly breath.

Then take ye good heed,
Who are Christ's indeed,
When the hearts of the nations shall fail them for fear:
For the prophets that lie
Shall then mightily cry,
And many shall say that the time draweth near:

But the Sun in the sky
Shall first sicken and die,
And the Moon shall withdraw her silvery light,
And the stars fall apace,
And vanish in space,
And the Heavens be extinguished in blackness of Night.

And then shall appear
Bright-shining and clear
The sign of Messiah uplifted on high;
He shall come in that hour
On the clouds with great power,
And all men shall know that Judgment is nigh.

The trumpet shall sound
Above and around,
And the mighty Archangel shall utter his voice,
And the dead shall come forth,
And the holy of earth
Shall be caught up in clouds, and for ever rejoice.

THE LAST JUDGMENT.

"He shall sit on the throne of his glory."

Methought it was the great dread day,
When Heaven and Earth did pass away,
And all things crumbled to decay.

Methought that men unguarded were,
And few imagined cause for fear,
Or dreamt that judgment-hour was near.

Methought th' Archangel's trump spake out
In one long loud deep dreadful note,
Which earth to'its very centre smote.

Methought the Son of Man appeared,
His sign a banner high upreared,
And all men saw him now, and feared.

Methought he was attended by
Ten thousand thousands of the sky,
All robed in glorious majesty.

Methought I heard Creation sigh,
And millions, as in agony,
For mercy, mercy, mercy, cry,

I saw men cast away their gold,
Which once so precious they did hold,
That for it life itself they sold;

I heard them wish the hills would fall,
I heard them to the mountains call,
To be to them a covering pall;

And they, who once were wont to mock,
When good men spake of judgment-shock,
Were scattered like a frightened flock:

And some, who used to say the snare
Should never catch them unaware,
Were now transfixed with blank despair;

And not a few, whom men did deem
To stand right high in God's esteem,
Awoke in terror from their dream.

Methought I heard a voice, and lo!
Earth opened wide—I saw below
The dead of ages, high and low.

Methought the mighty Ocean's bed
Was summoned to give up its dead,
And straightway all its waters fled.

I saw them come forth from the womb
Of earth and sea, their long long tomb,
A countless host, to hear their doom,

I looked, and lo! a great white throne!
The King of Glory sat thereon,
And now both Earth and Heaven had gone.

I looked again, and lo! the Man
Who framed redemption's blessèd plan,
Who loosed of sin and death the ban:

'Twas he who came down from on high,
Great Lord of earth, and sea, and sky,
To live, to suffer, and to die;

'Twas he, whose flesh the scourge had torn,
Whose brow was pierced with plaited thorn,
Whose back the heavy Cross had borne;

'Twas he, who knew the shame and pain
Of sin and death—but not the stain—
That men with God might live and reign;

'Twas he, the Man of sorrows, worn
With grief, with pain, with insult, scorn,
An outcast once, despised, forlorn;

Long by his interceding power
He had deferred the judgment-hour,
Lest God his vengeance should outpour;

'Twas he: but oh! how changèd now!
How fair his form! how bright his brow!
His eyes like living fire did glow!

Not one but now the Lord did know,
Not one but at his throne did bow,
Not one but prayed him save them now;

Yes, all were eager now to claim
His lineage, love, resemblance, name,
However great their former fame:

'Twas all too late!—the time had past,
When God would grant what sinners asked:
The tarrying Judge had come at last.

They stood before him; all did keep
Silence suspensive, awful, deep;
The Angels listened; men did weep.

I saw the books, wherein were read
The works of all, both quick and dead,
What each had done, or thought, or said;

The book, too, where th' elect were named,
Whose hearts the love of God inflamed,
Despised on earth, destroyed, defamed:

The shameful verdict was reversed,
Which blessed the vile, the holy cursed—
God's righteous law the Judge rehearsed.

As shepherds, who on moorland steep
Two mighty flocks apart do keep,
Know which be goats and which be sheep,

So he by instant vision knew
The natures of that motley crew,
The good, the bad, the false, the true.

He ranged them in a double band,
And these he placed on his right hand,
Those on his left were made to stand.

'Twas done : he turned him to his right,
And straight upon them shone a light,
As of the sun, pure, heavenly, bright;

And such a voice fell on my ear,
As ne'er 'twas mortal's lot to hear,
So kind, so soft, so sweet, so clear :

" Come ye,"—he said,—" my Father's blest,
" Enter with joy the heavenly rest,
" Prepared for you, by you possest :

" When I was hungry, food ye brought me,
" When I was thirsty, drink ye sought me,
" When I was naked, clothing wrought me ;

" When I was sick, then ye stood by me,
" When I was prisoned, ye came nigh me,
" A stranger, ye did not pass by me."

Amazed they heard the gracious word,
At last assured, with one accord
They ventured thus to' address their Lord :

" Lord, when saw we thee hungerèd?
" Or thirsty? or when sick,"—they said,—
" A stranger? naked? prisonèd?
" And to thy wants have ministrèd? "

To whom the King: "Nay, wonder not,
"Ye did on earth ye know not what,
"'Twas not by me unmarked, forgot;

"When some poor man your care aroused,
"Or when ye saw the stranger housed,
"Or injured innocence espoused,

"Or when ye gave the widow rest,
"Or clasped the orphan to your breast,
"Or called the Christian outcast Guest,

"Or cheered the sick man's silent room,
"Or lit the holy prisoner's gloom,
"Or rescued sinners from the tomb,

"'Twas *I* who then your care aroused,
"I was the stranger whom ye housed,
"Mine was the cause which ye espoused,

"'Twas I to whom ye gave the rest,
"In orphan children I was blest,
"I was the outcast, I the guest,

"For me ye wiped the dying brow,
"For me ye whispered kind and low,
"For me your knee in prayer did bow;

"These were my *brethren*, these did ye
"Hold precious; what in charity
"Ye did to them, ye did to ME."

He turned, and, with a dreadful frown,
And voice to righteous anger grown,
Those on his left did thus disown:

"Depart, ye cursèd, to the fire
"Prepared against the day of ire
"For Satan and his damnèd quire:

"I hungered, but no food ye brought me,
"I thirsted, but no drink ye sought me,
"Was naked, ye no clothing wrought me,

"When I was sick, ye stood not by me,
"A prisoner, ye did not come nigh me,
"I was a stranger, ye passed by me."

O'erwhelmed with terror and dismay,
They heard the dread anathema;
Then with vain effort to gainsay:

" Lord, when saw we thee hungerèd?
" Or thirsty! or when sick?—they said,—
" A stranger? naked? prisonèd?
" And have not to Thee ministrèd?"

Few words to these the Lord did deign,
The Lord who now had come to reign
And banish from him wicked men:

" What ye to but the humblest one
" Of these my *brethren* have not done,
" That, know, to ME ye have not done."

He spake, and, while he spake, all eyes
Stood steadfast fixed, filled with surprise
That God his servants thus should prize!

And now the Lord had told the doom
Of the vast people of the tomb,
These went to joy, and those to gloom.

THE PRINCE OF WALES IN A COURT OF JUSTICE.

"The throne is established by righteousness."

He spake his Royal word—
Gladly the people heard
 Their Prince was one
Who had not faithless been
To God, to wife, and Queen,
 And England's throne.

Though born of noblest race,
Destined for highest place,
 With riches blest,
Yet hath he greater fame
From an untarnished name,
 And with it rest.

Crowns, sceptres, robes of state,
The palace fair and great—
  These are not power:
His is the Sov'reignty,
Whose is the victory
  In judgment's hour.

God grant that, when he reign,
He still be without stain,
  Husband and wife
Guarding their wedded love,
Till they shall reign above
  In the *new* life.

RECOVERY FROM SICKNESS OF THE PRINCE OF WALES.

"Prayer was made without ceasing unto God for him."

"God save the Prince of Wales,"—
'Twas heard mid tears and wails
   Through all the land ;
   God's chastening hand
   Had prostrate laid
   The Royal head.

All feared the fatal hour,
Medicine had lost its power ;
   One hope alone
   From the High Throne,
   If *God* would spare
   The kingdom's Heir.

They prayed—a *Nation* prayed;
Soon was the fever stayed—
   His will, who gave
   Life, and can save,
   Whose sovereign sway
   All things obey.

Therefore, ye people, bring
Praises to God your King;
   Both high and low,
   Before him bow;
   He sits above
   Ruling in love.

NATIONAL THANKSGIVING FOR THE PRINCE OF WALES' RECOVERY.

"I will thank thee, for thou hast heard me, and art become my salvation."

To the great Cathedral dome
See the Royal cortége come,
Decked in gorgeous robes of state
Queen and Prince and Potentate;
Loud hosannas rend the air,
Loud thanksgivings everywhere:
See them now, with lowly gait,
Pass within the Temple-gate;
As before the Throne they kneel,
Sounds the organ's solemn peal,
Now ten thousand voices praise
God for health and length of days.

What oblations shall he bring
To the High and Heavenly King?
How most fitting thanks express
For great mercy in distress?
Ask the newly-fashioned clay
If it can the potter pay;
Gives the worm that crawls on earth
Aught to Him who gave it birth?
Princes on their golden throne
Cannot for their souls atone;
Christ alone the ransom paid,
Christ the deadly fever stayed.

Contrite hearts, devout desires,
Holy lives, our God requires;
Praise Him for His glorious might;
Praise Him for His love and light;
Praise Him for salvation given;
Praise Him for new life from Heaven;
Praise Him, for His chastening hand
Soon he took from off our land;
Praise Him, for He heard our prayer,
Healed the sick, dispelled our fear,
Praise Him, praise Him, praises bring
To our great and glorious King.

MARRIAGE OF THE PRINCESS LOUISE AND THE MARQUIS OF LORNE.

"His banner over me was love."

What is beauty, what is birth,
What is all the wealth of earth,
What the brightest costliest gem
In the monarch's diadem,

If the heart be sold for gain,
Marriage be but custom's chain,
Love be sacrificed to fame,
Freedom but an empty name?

Love cannot be bought or sold,
Love its fair love must enfold,
Love goes forth to seek its own
In the cot and on the throne.

Princess of our dear old land,
Worth like thine might well command
Kings and Princes to aspire
To thy hand with love's desire.

Thou to England's sons hast shown,
That man's seated on a throne,
Who hath virtue for a crown,
Whether fortune smile or frown.

England's glory! Scotland's pride!
Let the marriage knot be tied,
Plighted troth, and Book, and ring,
As for subject, so for king.

Thou, great God, who hast ordained
Marriage should be unconstrained,
Pour upon the noble pair
Gifts yet nobler and more rare.

Shine out, Sun, with glorious ray
On the happy wedding day;
Storms, your murmurs hoarse contain,
Not a cloud the welkin stain.

Breezes of the new-born Spring,
Sweetest odours with you bring;
Let the Earth her loveliest flowers
Yield from most delightsome bowers.

Lords and ladies, fine and fair,
Greet the newly-wedded pair;
Merriment and jocund fun
Round the festive circle run.

People all, in bright array,
Keep the joyous holiday:
Let the peasant with the peer
Join in good old English cheer.

THE UNIVERSITY BOAT-RACE OF 1872.

"*One* receiveth the prize."

Pull hard, my boys, pull hard,
'Tis not for vile reward,
 For muck of earth,
For gold or silver's worth;
 'Tis to obtain
A higher nobler gain,
 That deathless Fame,
Which none but spirits bold and brave can claim.

Pull harder yet, boys, pull,
And force the slender hull
 To cut her way
Right through the watery spray;
 Bravo! Well done!
"The Cam, the Cam has won,"
 With mighty roar
Thunder ten thousand tongues from shore to shore.

THE DEMON OF WAR.

"Destruction upon destruction."

The Fury waves her brand of war,
And calls her legions from afar;
" To arms," the maddened nations cry,
" On, on,—we conquer or we die."
Peace droops her head, and Commerce sighs,
And Culture languishes and dies.
I heard upon the rising gale
A mother's shriek, a widow's wail;
I saw a soldier carried past,
The blood of life was ebbing fast;
I saw a field, wherein were laid
Heaps upon heaps, unburied dead!
Famine and Pestilence were there,
The vulture hovered in the air,
Mankind had fled, the land was bare;
Yet still the Fury waved her brand,
And still fresh legions, sword in hand,
Killed and were killed—her dire command.

FRANCE AND PRUSSIA.

Written in 1870.

Head of France, thou didst not well
First to sound the battle-knell:
All the blood that shall be spilt
Will but add unto thy guilt.

Prussian monarch, hadst thou said
But *one word*, the countless dead
Would not have been strown in vain
On each bloody battle-plain.

Emperor and Monarch, hear—
There is One yet mightier;
He will judge you at his bar
For this wanton wicked war.

THE INSTABILITY OF EARTHLY GREATNESS.

"I went by, and lo! he was gone; I sought him, but his place could no where be found."

A little breath of wind, you know,
Into a tempest soon may grow,
And overthrow the sturdiest tree
In all its forest majesty;
So too the Princes of to-day
To-morrow may be nought but clay:
While yet upon their schemes they're bent,
There comes some little incident,
And changes all the government;
Their robe, their sceptre, and their crown
Soon to the dust are tumbled down;
Already on the vacant throne
There sits in state another one,
Who hears the huzzas long and loud
Of the ungrateful fickle crowd!

Yet do we see men every hour
Striving to build them some great tower,
Fancying to reign in mighty power;
Though scarcely is the wish obtained,
The tower finished, power gained,
Than comes the little shock, and oh!
A great, a startling overthrow!
The finished tower, 'tis no more,
Perished the man who had the power,
His reign has lasted scarce an hour!
   Such scenes of ruin and of woe,
Think you, no useful end can show?
Read them aright, they bid us know
Th' uncertainty of all below,
That, kindled with intense desire,
We may to greater heights aspire,
And in the *Heavens* seek an abode
Prepared and built for us by God.

THE REDS OF PARIS.

" Woe unto them."

Ye devilish crew,
If Hell itself such Demons hold as you,
Not brave to fight against your country's foe,
Brave only to inflict upon your country woe,
To pillage and to massacre her sons,
And point against an unarmed multitude your guns,
Haters of all that's noble and that's good,
Confederate with traitors, men defiled with blood,
Mouthing your curses against God most high,
As if ye had the strength th' Almighty to defy;
Ye would not bow to his correcting hand,
Know, then, He hath ten thousand scourges at command,
His thunder, and His lightning, and His rain,
The shock of earthquake, and the racking hurricane,
The choking heat, the scorching fiery glow,
And cold of Winter with its ice and frost and snow,

Blasting, and mildew, and the worm, and fly,
And clouds of countless locusts, darkening the sky,
    Famine, and Pestilence, and wild Despair,
And Idiotcy and Madness, Hell-delivered pair,
    And that last plague, in torment to expire,
Fearing worse torment of Gehenna's quenchless fire.

REFORMATION.

"The darkness is passing and the true light now shineth."

Hail! second Reformation, come at last,
To terminate the quarrels of the past,
To reconcile conflicting sects and schools,
And make them cast aside their senseless rules—
Those traps and stumbling-blocks by which so well
They've served the purpose of the Prince of Hell—
Decrees of Councils, Canons, Statutes, Laws,
Hair-splitting definitions without cause,
Tests, Articles, and Bulls, and such like stuff,
As if the Gospel-truths were not enough:
Christ dead and risen, Righteousness and Love,
Affections set on Christ and things above,
These things sufficed th' Apostles for a Creed,
These things sustained them in their hours of need,

For these the holy Martyrs lived and died,
With these all good men have been satisfied;
Strong in the faith, they fought the battle well,
And overthrew the mighty hosts of Hell,
And yet no steepled Churches were there then,
No vast endowments had those holy men,
They leaned not on the prop of any State,
Nor looked to Parliaments to make them great;
Poor and despised, but filled with God's own leaven,
With mighty power they led the way to Heaven,
Won souls to Christ, to heathen lands were sent;
This was their gain, *this* their emolument.

ON THE DEATH OF SIR CHARLES CLARKE.

"Thou shalt come to thy grave in a full age, like as a shock of corn cometh in his season."

Say, Colet, say, for whom has rung
The minstrel's harp that silent hung?
For whom essays he to prolong
His sweet but melancholy song?
What name to rescue from the gloom
That settles round the silent tomb?
O thou whose well-known healing power
Blessed thousands in affliction's hour,
Condemned alas! thyself to' endure
The ills, for others thou could'st cure;
I bring this tribute to thy grave,
'Tis little, but 'tis all I have;

For oft thy judgment would excuse
The trifling of my fitful Muse :
No more thy genial smile shall cheer
Our social feasts from year to year—
A constant guest, until at last
Thy manly frame was sinking fast;
Absent in body, not in will,
Thy Spirit hovered round us still.
Well did we know thy fost'ring care,
Well, too, thy love of talent rare,
With thee took part in classic lore,
With thee in play when school was o'er :
The noble Roman, who of old
With Lælius did sweet converse hold,
Yet sought some respite from his toil
Amid the Ocean's outcast spoil,
Collecting pebbles on the sand,
Where stretches Baiæ's pleasant strand :
So thou, too, on life's sunny shore
Didst sportive play, till day was o'er,
Till the dark billow, flowing fast,
O'ertook thee with its tide at last :
Alas! dear friend, to sooth our pain
Where shall we find thy like again ?

If medicine failed to do its part,
Yet never failed thy merry heart,
Never thy look, thy word, of love,
Never thy prayer to God above :
If naught availed, the pillow thou
Wouldst turn to cool the fevered brow.
All, all must die ; then blest are they
Who calmly meet the dreadèd day :
The bad a stubborn front oppose
To ruthless Fate's redoubled blows ;
Not so the good ; life's thread is spent,
The struggle's short, they die content :
Thou, like the full ripe corn which stands
Ready to fill the reaper's hands,
Didst to the sickle bow thy head,
And meekly join the holy dead.

This translation, from some Latin verses of the Rev. Dr. Kynaston, was made at the request of the late Mrs. Chilver, daughter of Sir Charles Clarke, a most kind and benevolent lady, who met her death a few years ago by a frightful accident on the South Eastern Railway, while her husband, an eminent medical man and philanthropist, who was sitting by her side, providentially escaped uninjured.

THE DAYS OF OUR AGE.

"The days of our age are threescore years and ten, and, though men be so strong that they come to fourscore years, yet is their strength then but labour and sorrow."

Whoso has lived to threescore years and ten
Has filled the term allowed to mortal men;
Whoso shall add yet half another score
Has, as his gain, sorrow and suffering sore;
Beyond these years a man may draw his breath,
But hardly lives—he hangs 'twixt life and death.
Lord, teach us, whatsoe'er our length of days,
Always to walk in thy most holy ways
That, when we shall have reached our journey's end,
Thou, as in life, in death be still our friend;
For, living *here*, we die; *there* we shall live
That deathless life which Christ alone can give.

ON A POOR MAN'S GRAVE.

"The Lord knoweth them that are His."

Hard was his path in life,
   Heavy the load he drew,
How heavy, and how hard,
   God only knew!

If, then, he seemed to thee
   A laggard in life's race,
Haply to God who knew
   He moved apace.

Easy thy path and smooth,
   Thy burden too is light,
Fear lest thy speed be not
   Speed in God's sight.

He laboured to the end,
 Thy life is not yet past,
See thou be found, as he
 Was at the *last*.

THE POWER OF GOD.

" With God all things are possible."

From the dead carcase of a forest beast
God's saint of old obtained a living feast,
And from a withered fig-tree Jesus gave
A lesson of the faith that's strong to save;
Thus God can give both food and faith, you see,
From beasts that perish and a withered tree!
Now He, who thus could dying men revive,
Can also make men, when they're dead, alive.

THE STEAM-ENGINE.

"The power of his might."

Seest thou yon engine ?   Had it not a vent,
Whereby the steam pent up within were spent,
'Twould burst its iron prison with loud roar,
And deal around Death and destruction sore ;
And so, when God doth with his holy fire
The inmost caverns of the heart inspire,
It too, in spite of every obstacle,
Makes itself felt, although invisible,
Yet not to strew the ground with piles of dead
Is the great Spirit sent down by our Head,
But to endow men with a higher life,
Still to be theirs after this mortal strife.

THE NEWS OF THE DAY.

"Good news from a far country."

"What news is there to-day?" said one to me:
"Important news, good Sir," quoth I, "for thee;
"Good news from Heaven!
"God's own Son given!
"For us he died! for us was raised!
"Through him we live! the Lord be praised!
"This is the news, which they who know
"No better have, or *wish*, I trow."

ON THE DEATH OF BISHOP PHILPOTTS.

Before the Lord called Philpotts to his rest,
He to vacate his see by man was prest:
The agèd Bishop yielded, and desired
A better see : 'twas granted—he *expired*.

TRANSLATION OF A LATIN EPIGRAM.

Trust God, pray oft, beware of sin, and be
Humble, and seek for peace, and high things flee,
Hear much, speak little, secrets keep, and spare
The weak, obey the strong, with equals bear,
Be earnest, faithful, to the needy nigh,
Thy gettings keep, bear all things, learn to die.

PART II.

TRANSLATIONS FROM THE ODES OF HORACE.

LIBER I.   CARMEN I.

Mæcenas atavis edite regibus,
O et præsidium et dulce decus meum,
Sunt quos curriculo pulverem Olympicum
Collegisse juvat, metaque fervidis
Evitata rotis palmaque nobilis.
Terrarum dominos evehit ad deos
Hunc, si mobilium turba Quiritium
Certat tergeminis tollere honoribus;
Illum, si proprio condidit horreo
Quicquid de Libycis verritur areis.
Gaudentem patrios findere sarculo
Agros Attalicis condicionibus
Numquam dimoveas, ut trabe Cypria
Myrtoum pavidus nauta secet mare.
Luctantem Icariis fluctibus Africum
Mercator metuens otium et oppidi

BOOK I.   ODE. I.

Mæcenas, sprung from line of ancient kings,
O both the strength and glory of my life,
There are whose joy is on th' Olympic course
To have swept along the dust, and shunned the goal
With glowing wheels, and won the noble palm.
Uplifted to the Gods, lords of the world,
This one, if the Quirites' fickle throng
Contend to' exalt to Honour's threefold height;
That one, if in his granary he has stored
All that is swept from Lybian threshing floors;
Whoso rejoices with his spade to cleave
His fathers' fields, by Attalus' wealth
Thou ne'er couldst move him, on a Cyprian beam,
Sailing with fear, to cut Myrtoan sea;
The South wind wrestling with the Icarian waves,
The merchant fearing praises the repose

Laudat rura sui : mox reficit rates
Quassas, indocilis pauperiem pati.
Est qui nec veteris pocula Massici
Nec partem solido demere de die
Spernit, nunc viridi membra sub arbuto
Stratus, nunc ad aquæ lene caput sacræ.
Multos castra juvant et lituo tubæ
Permixtus sonitus bellaque matribus
Detestata. Manet sub Jove frigido
Venator teneræ conjugis immemor,
Seu visa est catulis cerva fidelibus,
Seu rupit teretes Marsus aper plagas.
Me doctarum hederæ præmia frontium
Dis miscent superis, me gelidum nemus
Nympharumque leves cum Satyris chori
Secernunt populo, si neque tibias
Euterpe cohibet nec Polyhymnia
Lesboum refugit tendere barbiton.
Quodsi me lyricis vatibus inseres,
Sublimi feriam sidera vertice.

And scenery of his town; soon his wrecked raft
Refits, untutored poverty to bear;
There is who neither spurns old wine in cups,
Nor from the busy day to steal an hour,
His limbs now spread beneath green arbute-tree,
By gentle springhead now of sacred stream.
Many the camp delights, and trumpet's sound
With clarion commingled, and the wars
By mothers hated. Bides 'neath frosty sky
The huntsman, mindless of his tender wife,
Whether a doe his faithful hounds have viewed,
Or Marsian boar has burst the well-wrought nets:
Me ivy-wreath, the prize of learnèd brows,
Blends with the Gods above, me the cool grove
And airy Nymphs with Satyrs in the dance
Do sever from the people; if her pipes
Euterpe stay not, nor Pol'hymnia
Refuse to string the Lesbian maiden's lyre;
But if thou'lt graft me mid the lyric bards,
With upraised head I'll strike the stars of Heaven.

LIBER I.   CARMEN XI.

Tu ne quæsieris (scire nefas) quem mihi, quem tibi
Finem di dederint, Leuconoe, nec Babylonios
Temptaris numeros.   Ut melius, quicquid erit, pati,
Seu plures hiemes seu tribuit Juppiter ultimam,
Quæ nunc oppositis debilitat pumicibus mare
Tyrrhenum.   Sapias, vina liques et spatio brevi
Spem longam reseces.   Dum loquimur, fugerit invida
Ætas : carpe diem, quam minimum credula postero.

BOOK I.   ODE XI.

Thou should'st not seek—'tis sin to know—what end
    to thee, what end to me,
The Gods have given, Leuconoe; nor calculations of
    Chaldee
Should'st thou essay; far better bear, whate'er shall
    be, submissively,
Be it that Heaven more Winters gives, or this, the last
    that is to be,
Which even now with barrier cliffs doth break the sea
    of Tuscany;
Would'st thou be wise, filtrate the wines, and, as Life's
    span so brief must be,
Cut short long hope: e'en while we speak, Time will
    have fled invidiously;
Enjoy to-day, and trust as little as may be Futurity.

LIBER I.   CARMEN XIV.

O navis, referent in mare te novi
Fluctus.   O quid agis?   Fortiter occupa
    Portum.   Nonne vides ut
    Nudum remigio latus,

Et malus celeri saucius Africo
Antemnæque gemant, ac sine funibus
    Vix durare carinæ
    Possint imperiosius

Æquor.   Non tibi sunt integra lintea,
Non di quos iterum pressa voces malo.
    Quamvis Pontica pinus,
    Silvæ filia nobilis,

BOOK I.   ODE XIV.

O Ship, fresh-rising billows will bear thee back again
To the deep sea! What dost thou? O hold with might and main
  The harbour.   Seest thou not how bare
  Thy sides of oars to speed thee are,

Thy mast, too, sorely wounded with the swift hurricane
And sailyards groan; and, were't not for cables to sustain,
  Thy keel could scarcely now abide
  The more and more imperious tide?

There is not now to aid thee a yet untattered sail,
Nor Gods to' invoke when stricken again by adverse gale :
  For all that thou, a Pontic pine,
  The forest's child, of noble line,

Jactes et genus et nomen inutile,
Nil pictis timidus navita puppibus
    Fidit. Tu nisi ventis
    Debes ludibrium, cave.

Nuper sollicitum quæ mihi tædium,
Nunc desiderium curaque non levis,
    Interfusa nitentes
    Vites æquora Cycladas.

Vauntest a useless title and genealogy,
The fearful sailor trusts not in painted finery;
   O if thou art not bound to bear
   The mocking tempests, be thou ware.

Thou who of late didst cause me distressful weariness,
Now cause of anxious longing, and care not burdenless,
   Avoid the intermingling seas
   Mid those bright isles the Cyclades.

LIBER I. CARMEN XV.

Pastor cum tràheret per freta navibus
Idæis Helenen perfidus hospitam,
Ingrato celeris obruit otio
    Ventos ut caneret fera

Nereus fata : 'Mala ducis avi domum
Quam multo repetet Græcia milite,
Conjurata tuas rumpere nuptias
    Et regnum Priami vetus.

Heu heu, quantus equis, quantus adest viris
Sudor ! quanta moves funera Dardanæ
Genti. Jam galeam Pallas et ægida
    Currusque et rabiem parat.

BOOK I. ODE XV.

When that perfidious shepherd was dragging 'cross the sea
On board the ships of Ida the stranger Helene,
The Sea-god sank the swift winds in welcomeless repose,
    To sing the chant of destined woes:

" Thou art escorting homeward with evil augury
" Whom Græcia will demand back with countless soldiery,
" A sworn confederation to break thy nuptial vow,
    And Priam's old realm to lay low.

" Alas! what sweat for horses! what sweat for men's at hand!
" What carnage thou art stirring for all of Dardan land!
" E'en now doth Goddess Pallas her helmet, and her car,
    " Her ægis, and her rage prepare!

Nequiquam Veneris præsidio ferox
Pectes cæsariem grataque feminis
Imbelli cithara carmina divides,
    Nequiquam thalamo gravis

Hastas et calami spicula Gnosii
Vitabis strepitumque et celerem sequi
Aiacem : tamen heu serus adulteros
    Crines pulvere collines.

Non Laertiaden, exitium tuæ
Genti, non Pylium Nestora respicis ?
Urgent inpavidi te Salaminius
    Teucer, te Sthenclus sciens

Pugnæ, sive opus est imperitare equis,
Non auriga piger. Merionen quoque
Nosces. Ecce furit te reperire atrox
    Tydides melior patre ;

Quem tu, cervus uti vallis in altera
Visum parte lupum graminis inmemor,
Sublimi fugies mollis anhelitu,
    Non hoc pollicitus tuæ.

" In vain shalt thou, confiding in Love's protectorate,
" Comb out thy locks, and, pleasing a band effeminate,
" Blend with unwarlike harpings the song in harmony;
 " In vain to thy bedchamber flee,

" To shun the deadly lances, the barbs of Cretan reed,
" The battle-roar, and Ajax swift in pursuit to lead;
" However, though alas! late, thou thine adult'rous hair
 " Shalt thick with clotted dust besmear.

" Dost thou not Laerti'des, the scourge of all thy clan,
" Dost thou not agèd Nestor regard the Pylian man?
" A dauntless twain hot press thee—Teucer of Salamis,
 " And Sthenelus of skilled practise

" In battle, or, if need be to make the horses wheel,
" No laggard charioteer he! Merion too thou'lt feel!
" Lo! pitiless Tydides, a better than his sire,
 " To find thee burns with fierce desire;

" Whom thou—just as a stag flees a he-wolf it has seen
" Afar across the valley, unmindful of the green—
" Thy head upraised and panting, shalt flee in coward flight—
 " This was not to thy love thy plight!

Iracunda diem proferet Ilio
Matronisque Phrygum classis Achillei;
Post certas hiemes uret Achaicus
    Ignis Iliacas domos.'

"The anger of Achilles and all his fleet shall stay
" For Ilium and the matrons of Phrygia that day;
" Soon as the fixèd number of winters shall expire,
    " The Greeks shall burn Troy's homes with fire."

LIBER I.   CARMEN XXIV.

Quis desiderio sit pudor aut modus
Tam cari capitis? Præcipe lugubris
Cantus, Melpomene, cui liquidam pater
  Vocem cum cithara dedit.

Ergo Quintilium perpetuus sopor
Urget? cui Pudor et Justitiæ soror,
Incorrupta Fides, nudaque Veritas
  Quando ullum inveniet parem?

Multis ille bonis flebilis occidit,
Nulli flebilior quam tibi, Vergili.
Tu, frustra pius, heu non ita creditum
  Poscis Quintilium deos.

BOOK I.   ODE XXIV.

What bound to sorrow, or restraint should be
For one so dear? Begin, Melpomene,
The mournful chants, to whom th' Almighty Sire
Hath given with a liquid voice the lyre.

Doth, then, our friend th' eternal sleep oppress?
Faith uncorrupt, sister of Righteousness,
And Modesty, and naked Truth—ah! when
Shall they one like Quintilius find again?

Full many good men weep that he is gone,
Weep more than thou dost, Virgil, there is none;
In vain thy piety! not *so* was given
Quintilius, whom thou askest for from Heaven.

Quid si Threicio blandius Orpheo
Auditam moderere arboribus fidem,
Num vanæ redeat sanguis imagini,
    Quam virga semel horrida,

Non lenis precibus fata recludere,
Nigro compulerit Mercurius gregi?
Durum : sed levius fit patientia
    Quicquid corrigere est nefas.

What if more sweetly than the Thracian bard
Thou tun'dst the harp-strings and by trees wert heard?
Would then the blood run back to th' empty shade,
Which Mercury, whom no man can persuade

To burst the bar of Fate for soothing word,
Hath driven with dread wand to his black herd?
'Tis hard; but by endurance lighter grows
That which to alter God's law disallows.

LIBER I.   CARMEN XXXIV.

Parcus Deorum cultor et infrequens,
Insanientis dum sapientiæ
   Consultus erro, nunc retrorsum
      Vela dare atque iterare cursus

Cogor relictos. Namque Diespiter
Igni corusco nubila dividens
   Plerumque, per purum tonantis
      Egit equos volucremque currum,

Quo bruta tellus et vaga flumina,
Quo Styx et invisi horrida Tænari
   Sedes Atlanteusque finis
      Concutitur. Valet 'ima summis

BOOK I. ODE XXXIV.

A sparing and unfrequent devotee,
As long as from a mad philosophy
I took advice and wandered, now perforce
Backward I sail, and trace again the course
I had abandoned. For the Sire of Light,
Who most times cleaves the *clouds* with fire-flash bright,
Has driven thundering athwart the clear
His horses and his car in swift career,
Whereat the sluggish earth, the wandering flood,
And Styx, and hateful Tænarus' abode
Of subterranean horror, and withal
Th' Atlantic mountain, boundary of all,
Are shaken. The Almighty Power can make
Things that are highest lowest places take,

Mutare et insignem attenuat Deus,
Obscura promens; hinc apicem rapax
   Fortuna cum stridore acuto
     Sustulit, hic posuisse gaudet.

And the distinguished man he wears away,
Bringing obscure things forth to light of day :
Fortune from *this* man, snatching at her prey,
Bears with shrill whirr the diadem away,
Here having set it, glories in her sway.

LIBER II. CARMEN XVI.

Otium divos rogat in patenti
Prensus Ægæo, simul atra nubes
Condidit lunam neque certa fulgent
    Sidera nautis;

Otium bello furiosa Thrace,
Otium Medi pharetra decori,
Grosphe, non gemmis neque purpura ve-
    nale neque auro.

Non enim gazæ neque consularis
Summovet lictor miseros tumultus
Mentis et curas laqueata circum
    Tecta volantis.

BOOK II. ODE XVI.

Peace—asks the man from Heaven in prayer
Caught in the broad seas unaware,
When a black cloud the moon doth veil,
And no sure stars shine as they sail:

Peace—Thrace to war by Furies borne;
Peace—Medes whom quiver doth adorn;
'Tis not for gems, 'tis not for gold,
'Tis not for purple, Grosphus, sold.

Not wealth, nor consul's axeman may
Drive those tumultuous stirs away
Which vex the soul, and cares whose flight
Is round the fretted ceiling's height.

Vivitur parvo bene, cui paternum
Splendet in mensa tenui salinum
Nec leves somnos timor aut cupido
    Sordidus aufert.

Quid brevi fortes jaculamur ævo
Multa? quid terras alio calentes
Sole mutamus? patriæ quis exul
    Se quoque fugit?

Scandit æratas vitiosa navis
Cura nec turmas equitum relinquit,
Ocior cervis et agente nimbos
    Ocior Euro.

Lætus in præsens animus quod ultra est
Oderit curare et amara lento
Temperet risu : nihil est ab omni
    Parte beatum.

Abstulit clarum cita mors Achillem,
Longa Tithonum minuit senectus,
Et mihi forsan, tibi quod negarit,
    Porriget hora.

That man lives well off scanty hoard,
For whom upon a humble board
A salt-cellar gleams splendidly,
The heirloom of his ancestry,
Nor fear nor sordid avarice
Takes gentle slumbers from his eyes.

Wherefore do we, in our short day,
Aim at so much with bold essay?
Why seek lands warmed with other ray?
Who, from his country banishèd,
Hath also from his own self fled?

Corroding care climbs ships of brass,
Nor lets the troops of horsemen pass,
More swift than antelopes, more swift
Than winds which chase the stormy drift.

If joyful be our present state,
The mind far distant cares should hate,
And temper with a careless laugh
The bitter cup it hath to quaff!
Nothing exists which doth possess
On every side true happiness.

THE SPIRIT AND THE MUSE.

Te greges centum Siculæque circum
Mugiunt vaccæ, tibi tollit hinnitum
Apta quadrigis equa, te bis Afro
    Murice tinctæ

Vestiunt lanæ : mihi parva rura et
Spiritum Graiæ tenuem Camenæ
Parca non mendax dedit et malignum
    Spernere vulgus.

Quick Death cut short Achilles' fame,
Long age diminished Tithon's name,
And peradventure time to me
Will stretch what it denies to thee.

A hundred flocks and lowing kine
Of true Sicilian breed are thine ;
The mare lifts high her neigh for thee
Fit for the car of victory ;
Twice steeped in Afric's purple dye
The wools which are thy vesture : I
A little country farm received
From Destiny who ne'er deceived,
And the soft breath of Grecian song,
Aye, and to spurn the spiteful throng.

LIBER II.   CARMEN XVIII.

Non ebur neque aureum
Mea renidet in domo lacunar,
　　Non trabes Hymettiæ
Premunt columnas ultima recisas
　　Africa, neque Attali
Ignotus heres regiam occupavi,
　　Nec Laconicas mihi
Trahunt honestæ purpuras clientæ.
　　At fides et ingeni
Benigna vena est, pauperemque dives
　　Me petit : nihil supra
Deos lacesso nec potentem amicum
　　Largiora flagito,
Satis beatus unicis Sabinis,
　　Truditur dies die,
Novæque pergunt interire lunæ :

BOOK II. ODE XVIII.

No iv'ry, nor golden gleam
In my house glitters from a panelled ceiling-beam;
    No timbers from Hymettus brought
Press columns in the quarries of far Afric wrought;
    Nor yet from Attalus who reigned
Have I, an unknown heir, a regal house obtained;
    Nor of Laconian wool for me
Do noble maidens weave rich purple drapery;
    Yet faith and genius are to me,
A kindly-flowing vein; and, though so poor I be,
    The rich man seeks me; for no more
I importune the Gods, nor from my friend in power
    More liberal gifts do I require:
Enough the blessing of my farm, my one desire.
    Day ever pushes onward day,
And newly-risen moons hasten to pass away;

Tu secanda marmora
Locas sub ipsum funus et sepulcri
    Immemor struis domos
Marisque Bais obstrepentis urges
    Summovere litora,
Parum locuples continente ripa.
    Quid quod usque proximos
Revellis agri terminos et ultra
    Limites clientium
Salis avarus? Pellitur paternos
    In sinu ferens deos
Et uxor et vir sordidosque natos.
    Nulla certior tamen
Rapacis Orci sede destinata
    Aula divitem manet
Erum. Quid ultra tendis? Æqua tellus
    Pauperi recluditur
Regumque pueris, nec satelles Orci
    Callidum Promethea
Revexit auro captus : hic superbum
    Tantalum atque Tantali
Genus coercet, hic levare functum
    Pauperem laboribus
Vocatus atque non vocatus audit.

Thou, though so near the fun'ral gloom,
Dost order marbles to be cut, and, of the tomb
    Not mindful, palaces dost found!
And, where the sea makes Baiæ with a roar resound,
    Thou hurriest to remove the shore,
Not rich enough, because the bank confines thee sore!
    Why add that, at the boundary,
Thou thrustest back the landmarks, and beyond where lie
    The limits of thy clients' land
Thou leapest avaricious! Lo! an outcast band
    The wife and husband, on their breast
Bearing their fathers' Gods and ragged children prest!
    And yet no hall more certainly
Awaits the rich lord than the destined boundary
    Of ravenous Hell! Ah! wherefore try
To stretch to yonder distance? With strict equity
    Earth opens to the poor as well
As to the sons of kings. The satellite of Hell,
    For all Prometheus' subtlety,
Did not convey him back, captured by gold. 'Tis he
    Keeps haughty Tantalus, and all
The race of Tantalus confined: 'tis he withal
    Who, when the poor his work has done,
Invoked or not invoked to give relief, is won.

LIBER III. CARMEN XVI.

Inclusam Danaen turris aenea
Robustæque fores et vigilum canum
Tristes excubiæ munierant satis
    Nocturnis ab adulteris

Si non Acrisium virginis abditæ
Custodem pavidum Juppiter et Venus
Risissent: fore enim tutum iter et patens
    Converso in pretium deo.

Aurum per medios ire satellites
Et perrumpere amat saxa potentius
Ictu fulmineo: concidit auguris
    Argivi domus, ob lucrum

BOOK III. ODE XVI.

Imprisoned Danae, brazen tower,
Oak doors, and watch-dogs, sentry sour,
Had been sufficient to secure
From every nightly paramour,
Had not great Jove, and Goddess Love,
Laughed at Acrisius from above,
Guarding with fear the hidden maid;
A broad safe road, they saw, was made—
The God became the gold he paid.
Gold through the midst of troops will go,
And bursts through rocks with mightier blow
Than thunderstroke. The Argive seer
Perished with all that he held dear,
Gain plunged him in that gulf of woe:
The Macedonian hero, too,
Cleft right in twain the wallèd town
And brought his royal rivals down

Demersa exitio; diffidit urbium
Portas vir Macedo et subruit æmulos
Reges muneribus; munera navium
    Sævos inlaqueant duces.

Crescentem sequitur cura pecuniam
Majorumque fames. Jure perhorrui
Late conspicuum tollere verticem,
    Mæcenas, equitum decus.

Quanto quisque sibi plura negaverit
Ab dis plura feret; nil cupientium
Nudus castra peto et transfuga divitum
    Partes linquere gestio,

Contemptæ dominus splendidior rei
Quam si quicquid arat impiger Apulus
Occultare meis dicerer horreis,
    Magnas inter opes inops.

Puræ rivus aquæ silvaque jugerum
Paucorum et segetis certa fides meæ
Fulgentem imperio fertilis Africæ
    Fallit sorte beatior.

By secret gifts ; gifts often are
To the fierce naval chief a snare.
When money grows, soon will succeed
Care, and for larger things a greed ;
With reason I have had great dread
Of lifting up on high my head,
To be conspicuous far and wide,
Mæcenas, of the knights the pride.
The more each man himself deny,
The more shall he bear from on high ;
Naked I seek the camp of men
Who are not covetous of gain,
And, a deserter in the fight,
The rich man's side leave with delight.
With far more splendour do I shine,
While a contemned estate is mine,
Than were my barns said to contain
All that immense amount of grain
The brisk Apulians possess—
'Mid all my treasures treasureless.
A brook of water pure and good,
Just a few acres too of wood,
A tilth which will sure crops afford,
(Although the bright Imperial Lord

Quamquam nec Calabræ mella ferunt apes,
Nec Læstrygonia Bacchus in amphora
Languescit mihi, nec pinguia Gallicis
　　Crescunt vellera pascuis,

Importuna tamen pauperies abest
Nec, si plura velim, tu dare deneges.
Contracto melius parva cupidine
　　Vectigalia porrigam,

Quam si Mygdoniis regnum Alyattei
Campis continuem. Multa petentibus
Desunt multa: bene est, cui deus optulit
　　Parca quòd satis est manu.

Of fertile Afric know it not)
Indeed is a far happier lot.
I grant that no Calabrian bee
Produces honeycombs for me,
Nor yet in Læstrygonian jar
Bacchus grows mellow, nor afar
In Gallic pasture-lands increase
Fat sheep with their enormous fleece;
Yet incommodious poverty
Keeps at a distance far from me,
Nor, if I wished a larger store,
Wouldst thou refuse to give me more.
Better contract my wants, that *so*
My little revenue may grow,
Then if I Mygdon's plains obtained
With those where Alyattes reigned.
The men, who seek a mighty deal,
Are sure a mighty want to feel;
'Tis well to whom the God of Heaven
With sparing hand enough hath given.

LIBER III.   CARMEN XVIII.

Faune, Nympharum fugientum amator,
Per meos finis et aprica rura
Lenis incedas abeasque parvis
  Æquus alumnis,

Si tener pleno cadit hædus anno,
Larga nec desunt Veneris sodali
Vina crateræ, vetus ara multo
  Fumat odore.

Ludit herboso pecus omne campo,
Cum tibi nonæ redeunt Decembres;
Festus in pratis vacat otioso
  Cum bove pagus;

BOOK III.   ODE XVIII.

O Faunus, wooer of the Nymphs which flee,
Propitious step thou through my boundary
And sunny fields, and, ere thou dost depart,
A blessing to the little lambs impart,

If, at the year's close, a young kid is killed,
And with large draughts of wine the bowl is filled,
Comrade of Venus, and much sweet perfume
The ancient altar smoking doth consume :

Plays all the flock upon the grassy plain,
When thy December's Nones come round again ;
Feasting in meadows, from their labour cease
The villagers; the ox, too, takes his ease.

Inter audaces lupus errat agnos ;
Spargit agrestis tibi silva frondes ;
Gaudet invisam pepulisse fossor
　　Ter pede terram.

Among the daring lambs the he-wolf goes,
The forest at thy feet the wild leaves throws,
Glad is the ditcher three times with his feet
The surface of the hated earth to beat.

LIBER III. CARMEN XXIII.

Cælo supinas si tuleris manus
Nascente luna, rustica Phidyle,
   Si ture placaris et horna
   Fruge lares avidaque porca

Nec pestilentem sentiet Africum
Fecunda vitis nec sterilem seges
   Rubiginem aut dulces alumni
   Pomifero grave tempus anno.

Nam quæ nivali pascitur Algido
Devota quercus inter et ilices
   Aut crescit Albanis in herbis
   Victima, pontificum secures

BOOK III.   ODE XXIII.

If upward to the Heaven thy hands thou lift,
When the moon rises, O thou maid of thrift,
If frankincense and this year's grain appease,
Aye, and a greedy swine, the Images,
Nor will the fruitful vine the pestilence,
Wafted by Southern blast, experience,
Nor corn the sterile rust, nor darling flock
The apple-bearing season's deadly shock:
For the devoted victim which is fed,
Where snowy Algidus uplifts its head,
Betwixt the oaks and ilex-trees, or thrives
In Alban grasses, shall the Pontiffs' knives

Cervice tinguet : te nihil attinet
Temptare multa cæde bidentium
    Parvos coronantem marino
    Rore deos fragilique myrto.

Immunis aram si tetigit manus,
Non sumptuosa blandior hostia
    Mollivit aversos penates
    Farre pio et saliente mica.

Dye with its neck. Naught doth it thee avail
By shedding blood of many beasts to' assail
Thy little Gods, if but with rosemary
Thou crown them, and the fragile myrtle tree.
If pure the hand upon the altar laid,
No costly victim makes it more persuade,
It soothes th' averted Gods to turn again
By mite of crackling salt and holy grain.

LIBER III.   ODE XXIX.

Tyrrhena regum progenies, tibi
Non ante verso lene merum cado
    Cum flore, Mæcenas, rosarum et
        Pressa tuis balanus capillis

Jamdudum apud me est.   Eripe te moræ,
Nec semper udum Tibur et Æfulæ
    Declive contempleris arvum et
        Telegoni juga parricidæ.

Fastidiosam desere copiam et
Molem propinquam nubibus arduis ;
    Omitte mirari beatæ
        Fumum et opes strepitumque Romæ.

BOOK III.　ODE XXIX.

Offspring of Tuscan kings, for thee
There long ago has been with me
An unbroached cask of mellow wine,
With bloom of roses fresh and fine,
And balsam for those locks of thine:

Then haste to tear thee from delay,
Nor always Tibur's damp survey,
Æfula's slope, and the hill-side
Of Teleg'nus the parricide.

Leave scornful plenty and the pile,
Built to the lofty clouds, awhile;
Cease from admiring Rome's blest store—
Its smoke, its substance, and its roar.

Plerumque gratæ divitibus vices
Mundæque parvo sub lare pauperum
    Cenæ sine aulæis et ostro
        Sollicitam explicuere frontem.

Jam clarus occultum Andromedæ pater
Ostendit ignem, jam procyon furit
    Et stella vesani leonis,
        Sole dies referente siccos ;

Jam pastor umbras cum grege languido
Rivumque fessus quærit et horridi
    Dumeta Silvani, caretque
        Ripa vagis taciturna ventis.

Tu civitatem quis deceat status
Curas et urbi sollicitus times
    Quid Seres et regnata Cyro
        Bactra parent Tanaisque discors.

Prudens futuri temporis exitum
Caliginosa nocte premit deus,
    Ridetque si mortalis ultra
        Fas trepidat. Quod adest memento

Most times the rich like change of lot
And clean repasts 'neath poor man's cot,
Arras apart and purple glow,
Are wont to smooth the anxious brow.

Already bright Andromed's sire
Shows to the front his hidden fire;
Raves Leo's star, and Procyon burns,
The Sun with days of drought returns;

The weary swain with languid sheep
Seeks shady brook and thickets deep
Of rough Silvanus; far away
From the still bank the breezes stray.

Thy care—what suits the country best,
And for the city thou'rt distrest,
On what the Seres are intent,
What Bactra, Cyrus' government,
And Tanais with discord rent.

Wisely th' event of time to come
God buries in a murky gloom,
And smiles if mortal man doth fear

Componere æquus : cetera fluminis
Ritu feruntur, nunc medio alveo
    Cum pace delabentis Etruscum
    In mare, nunc lapides adesos

Stirpesque raptas et pecus et domos
Volventis una, non sine montium
    Clamore vicinæque silvæ,
    Cum fera diluvies quietos

Inritat amnes. Ille potens sui
Lætusque deget, cui licet in diem
    Dixisse 'Vixi : cras vel atra
    Nube polum pater occupato

Vel sole puro ; non tamen irritum
Quodcumque retro est efficiet, neque
    Diffinget infectumque reddet
    Quod fugiens semel hora vexit.'

Fortuna sævo læta negotio et
Ludum insolentem ludere pertinax
    Transmutat incertos honores,
    Nunc mihi, nunc alii benigna.

Beyond what's right, Mind, what is near
Adjust with calmness : all besides
Is borne stream-fashion ; now it glides
With peaceful channel to the sea,
Now rolls along impetuously
Trunks hurried headlong, homesteads, flocks,
The mountains sound and neighb'ring wood,
When quiet rivers the wild flood
Infuriates. That man self shall sway
And joyful dwell, who can each day
Say, 'I have lived; or with black cloud
To-morrow's sky the Sire shall shroud,
Or else—clear sunshine; yet not vain
That which is past, nor forged again
Nor yet unmade a single thing
Time once hath wafted on his wing.'

Rejoicing in her cruel trade,
Strange freak plays Fortune, stubborn jade !
Shifts fickle honours to and fro,
Now kind to me, to others now :
I praise her while she stays, but, if
She takes swift wing, resign her gift,
I wrap my virtue round my breast,

LIBER IV.   CARMEN VII.

Diffugere nives, redeunt jam gramina campis
  Arboribusque comæ;
Mutat terra vices, et decrescentia ripas
  Flumina prætereunt;
Gratia cum Nymphis geminisque sororibus audet
  Ducere nuda choros.
Immortalia ne speres, monet annus et almum
  Quæ rapit hora diem.
Frigora mitescunt Zephyris, ver proterit æstas
  Interitura, simul
Pomifer autumnus fruges effuderit, et mox
  Bruma recurrit iners.
Damna tamen celeres reparant cælestia lunæ;
  Nos ubi decidimus

BOOK IV.   ODE VII.

The snows have fled away; now grass comes to the plain,
    And to the trees their leaves again ;
Earth alternates her changes, and subsiding low
    Along their banks the rivers flow ;
The Grace, joined with the Nymphs, and her twin sisters dare
    To lead the choral dances bare :
" Hope not for things immortal"—seems the year to say,
    And th' hour which speeds the genial day;
Cold softens with the Zephyrs, Summer treads on Spring,
    To pass away, when Autumn bring
His apples and the fruits he pours profusely ; then
    Dull Winter soon runs round again ;
Yet losses in the Heavens quickly the moons repair,
    We, when we sink to that place, where

Quo pater Æneas, quo Tullus dives et Ancus,
　　Pulvis et umbra sumus.
Quis scit an adiciant hodiernæ crastina summæ
　　Tempora di superi?
Cuncta manus avidas fugient heredis, amico
　　Quæ dederis animo.
Cum semel occideris et de te splendida Minos
　　Fecerit arbitria,
Non, Torquate, genus, non te facundia, non te
　　Restituet pietas.
Infernis neque enim tenebris Diana pudicum
　　Liberat Hippolytum,
Nec Lethæa valet Theseus abrumpere caro
　　Vincula Pirithoo.

The good Æneas, Ancus, and rich Tullus be,
　　No more than dust and shade are we!
Who knows if Heaven will to the sum of this day give
　　To-morrow's hours to thee to live?
All will escape the greedy fingers of a grasping heir
　　Thou hast given to thine own soul dear:
When once thou'rt dead, and Minos hath pronounced on thee
　　Judgment in all its majesty,
Not thy descent, nor eloquence, Torquatus, nor
　　Thy piety shall thee restore:
For even Dian frees not chaste Hippolytus
　　From gloom of nether Tartarus,
Nor yet is Theseus able Lethe's chains to tear
　　From off Pirithous, though dear.

LIBER IV. CARMEN VIII.

Donarem pateras grataque commodus,
Censorine, meis æra sodalibus,
Donarem tripodas, præmia fortium
Graiorum, neque tu pessima muncrum
Ferres, divite me scilicet artium
Quas aut Parrhasius protulit aut Scopas,
Hic saxo, liquidis ille coloribus
Sollers nunc hominem ponere, nunc deum.
Sed non hæc mihi vis, nec tibi talium
Res est aut animus deliciarum egens.
Gaudes carminibus; carmina possumus
Donare et pretium dicere muneri.
Non incisa notis marmora publicis,
Per quæ spiritus et vita redit bonis

BOOK IV.   ODE VIII.

Gifts of goblets and bronzes I fain would bestow
With liberal hand on the friends whom I know—
Gifts of tripods, the prizes in Greece of the brave—
Nor should'st thou, Censorinus, the worst present have,
If forsooth I were rich in the arts first made known
By Parrhasius and Scopas, who, *this* one in stone,
By soft colours *that* one, with wonderful merit,
Now fashioned a man, and now the great Spirit.
But this power I have not; nor are thy affairs
Nor thy spirit in need of such delicate wares;
Thou delightest in song, and song we have power
To bestow, and the value to fix of the dower:
Not marbles engraved with inscriptions of State,
Which restore life and breath to good captains and great

Post mortem ducibus, non celeres fugæ,
Rejectæque retrorsum Hannibalis minæ,
Non incendia Carthaginis impiæ
Ejus, qui domita nomen ab Africa
Lucratus rediit, clarius indicant
Laudes quam Calabræ Pierides : neque,
Si chartæ sileant quod bene feceris,
Mercedem tuleris. Quid foret Iliæ
Mavortisque puer, si taciturnitas
Obstaret meritis invida Romuli?
Ereptum Stygiis fluctibus Æacum
Virtus et favor et lingua potentium
Vatum divitibus consecrat insulis.
Dignum laude virum Musa vetat mori,
Cælo Musa beat. Sic Jovis interest
Optatis epulis impiger Hercules,
Clarum Tyndaridæ sidus ab infimis
Quassas eripiunt æquoribus rates,
Ornatus viridi tempora pampino
Liber vota bonos ducit ad exitus.

When death overtakes them, nor yet the swift flight,
When Hannibal's threats were flung back on the wight,
Not impious Carthage, lit up in a blaze,
Point out with more clearness *his* glorious praise,
Who from Africa conquered obtained him a name,
Than the Muse of the man of Calabrian fame.
If parchments were silent of deeds bravely done,
No meed wouldst thou bear. Where would be the son
Of Ilia and Mavors, if silence withstood
With its envy the King whose deserts were so good?
Was Æacus snatched from the Stygian wave?
'Tis the virtue, the favour, the tongue strong to save,
Of *baras* which enshrine in the isles of the blest;
'Tis the Muses forbid him to die like the rest,
Who is worthy of praise; 'tis the Muses bestow
A blessing in Heaven; brave Hercules *so*
Hath a place at Jove's feast which he yearned for below;
It is *so* that the bright star, the Tyndaridæ,
The shattered bark rescues from depths of the sea;
It is *so*, the green vine-leaf adorning his brow,
That Liber conducts to good issues the vow.

T

EPODON LIBER.   CARMEN I.

Ibis Liburnis inter alta navium,
    Amice, propugnacula,
Paratus omne Cæsaris periculum
    Subire, Mæcenas, tuo.
Quid nos? quibus te vitâ si superstite
    Jucunda, si contra, gravis,
Utrumne jussi persequemur otium,
    Non dulce, ni tecum simul,
An hunc laborem mente laturi, decet
    Qua ferre non molles viros?
Feremus et te vel'per Alpium juga
    Inhospitalem et Caucasum,
Vel occidentis usque ad ultimum sinum
    Forti sequemur pectore.

EPODE. I.

In light Liburnian galleys thou, my friend, shalt go,
   'Mid the tall vessels armed from stern to prow,
Ready, whatever danger Cæsar shall confront,
   With danger to thyself to bear the brunt:
How is 't with us? to whom, if life to thee remain,
   Life is a pleasure, otherwise a pain:
Shall we, as bidden, still pursue a tranquil ease,
   Which charms not, save with thee to make it please?
Or shall we bear this trial, minded as 'tis right
   That men who're not effeminate should fight?
Bear it we will—and either 'cross the Alpine peak,
   And Caucasus inhospitably bleak,
Or even to the utmost coast-bend of the West,
   Thee we will follow with courageous breast:

Roges, tuum labore quid juvem meo
  Inbellis ac firmus parum :
Comes minore sum futurus in metu,
  Qui maior absentis habet;
Ut assidens inplumibus pullis avis
  Serpentium allapsus timet
Magis relictis, non, ut adsit, auxili
  Latura plus praesentibus.
Libenter hoc et omne militabitur
  Bellum in tuae spem gratiae,
Non ut juvencis illigata pluribus
  Aratra nitantur mea,
Pecusve Calabris ante sidus fervidum
  Lucana mutet pascuis,
Neque ut superni villa candens Tusculi
  Circaea tangat moenia.
Satis superque me benignitas tua
  Difavit : haut paravero
Quod aut avarus ut Chremes terra premam,
  Discinctus aut perdam nepos.

Dost ask how thy exertion I by mine can back,
　When I'm unwarlike, aye, and firmness lack?
In thy companionship, in less fear I shall be
　Which sways the absent more imperiously,
Just as a bird that sits beside her unfledged brood,
　When they are left, feels more disquietude
For serpents gliding towards them, though, if she were near,
　She would not in their presence more help bear:
Gladly we'll serve in this, and every war's campaign,
　Hoping thereby thy favour to obtain;
Not that, more numerous heifers to the traces bound,
　My ploughs may thrust them through and through the ground;
Nor that my flock may leave, when the hot star's at hand,
　Calabria for Lucanian pasture-land;
Nor that a glist'ning villa may adjoin the town,
　Built on a hill, which Circe's ramparts crown:
Enough, yea, too much has thy bounty in the past
　Enriched me; I'd not have a store amassed
To hide, like avaricious Chremes, in a pit,
　Or, like a spendthrift child, waste every bit.

EPODON LIBER.   CARMEN II.

Beatus ille qui procul negotiis,
    Ut prisca gens mortalium,
Paterna rura bobus exercet suis
    Solutus omni fenore,
Neque excitatur classico miles truci
    Neque horret iratum mare,
Forumque vitat et superba civium
    Potentiorum limina.
Ergo aut adulta vitium propagine
    Altas maritat populos,
Aut in reducta valle mugientium
    Prospectat errantes greges,
Inutilisque falce ramos amputans
    Feliciores inserit,

EPODE II.

'Happy the man, who from all business far away,
   Like mortals born in ancient day,
Upturns his fathers' broadlands with his own good steers,
   Freed wholly from usurious fears,
And is not roused by the fierce trumpet's call to war,
   Nor dreads the angry ocean's roar,
And shuns the forum, and the proud and haughty door
   Of citizens of too great power:
Therefore the adult layer of the vine-trees ho
   Marries to some tall poplar tree,
Or views, in some secluded valley bellowing,
   His herds of oxen wandering.
And, lopping unproductive branches with his knife,
   Grafts others in more rich with life,

EPODON LIBER.   CARMEN II.

Beatus ille qui procul negotiis,
　　Ut prisca gens mortalium,
Paterna rura bobus exercet suis
　　Solutus omni fenore,
Neque excitatur classico miles truci
　　Neque horret iratum mare,
Forumque vitat et superba civium
　　Potentiorum limina.
Ergo aut adulta vitium propagine
　　Altas maritat populos,
Aut in reducta valle mugientium
　　Prospectat errantes greges,
Inutilisque falce ramos amputans
　　Feliciores inserit,

EPODE II.

'Happy the man, who from all business far away,
    Like mortals born in ancient day,
Upturns his fathers' broadlands with his own good steers,
    Freed wholly from usurious fears,
And is not roused by the fierce trumpet's call to war,
    Nor dreads the angry ocean's roar,
And shuns the forum, and the proud and haughty door
    Of citizens of too great power :
Therefore the adult layer of the vine-trees he
    Marries to some tall poplar tree,
Or views, in some secluded valley bellowing,
    His herds of oxen wandering.
And, lopping unproductive branches with his knife,
    Grafts others in more rich with life,

Aut pressa puris mella condit amphoris
    Aut tondet infirmas oves :
Vel cum decorum mitibus pomis caput
    Autumnus agris extulit,
Ut gaudet insitiva decerpens pira,
    Certantem et uvam purpuræ,
Qua muneretur te, Priape, et te, pater
    Silvane, tutor finium.
Libet jacere modo sub antiqua ilice,
    Modo in tenaci gramine.
Labuntur altis interim ripis aquæ,
    Queruntur in silvis aves,
Fontesque lymphis obstrepunt manantibus,
    Somnos quod invitet leves,
At cum tonantis annus hibernus Jovis
    Imbres nivesque comparat,
Aut trudit acris hinc et hinc multa cane
    Apros in obstantis plagas,
Aut amite levi rara tendit retia,
    Turdis edacibus dolos,
Pavidumque leporem et advenam laqueo gruem
    Jucunda captat præmia;
Quis non malarum, quas amor curas habet,
    Hæc inter obliviscitur ?

Or pressing honey stows it in pure jars to keep,
    Or shears his flock of feeble sheep :
Or soon as Autumn, decked with those ripe fruits he yields,
    Uplifts his head throughout the fields,
How glad is he, while picking off th' ingrafted pear,
    Or grapes, with purple to compare,
A gift for thee, Priapus, and for thee, Silvan,
    Of boundaries the guardian.
Him listeth now to lie beneath some old oak tree,
    Now on the matted grass to be :
Glide on the waterbrooks meanwhile, the banks are high,
    Birds warble in the shrubbery,
And fountains sound an echo to the trickling stream,
    Inviting slumber's airy dream.
But when in Winter-time Jove thunders in the air
    The rains and snow-storms to prepare,
He drives fierce boars from here and there with many a hound
    Into the toils which stop their bound,
Or, with smooth pole outstretching wide the fine-wrought nets,
    For greedy fieldfares snares he sets,
And hunts the timorous hare, and traps the foreign crane,
    Delightful quarries these to gain !
Who does not 'mid such scenes forget the cursèd cares
    Which amorous courtship with it bears ?

Quodsi pudica mulier in partem juvet
  Domum atque dulcis liberos,
Sabina qualis aut perusta solibus
  Pernicis uxor Apuli,
Sacrum vetustis extruat lignis focum
  Lassi sub adventum viri,
Claudensque textis cratibus lætum pecus
  Distenta siccet ubera,
Et horna dulci vina promens dolio
  Dapes inemptas apparet :
Non me Lucrina juverint conchylia
  Magisve rhombus aut scari,
Siquos Eois intonata fluctibus
  Hiemps ad hoc vertat mare ;
Non Afra avis descendat in ventrem meum,
  Non attagen Ionicus
Jucundior quam lecta de pinguissimis
  Oliva ramis arborum,
Aut herba lapathi prata amantis et gravi
  Malvæ salubres corpori,
Vel agna festis cæsa terminalibus
  Vel hædus creptus lupo.
Has inter epulas ut juvat pastas oves
  Videre properantes domum,

But if a modest housewife helps to take her share
    Both with the house and children dear—
Just like the Sabine's spouse, or, burnt with blazing sun,
    She of the quick Apulian—
Piles high upon the sacred hearth old logs to cheer
    Her tired husband coming near,
And, shutting up the joyful flock in wattled pens,
    Their milk-distended udders drains,
And, drawing vintage of the year from luscious jar,
    An unbought banquet doth prepare,
Then *I* should not the oysters from the Lucrine bar,
    Nor turbot more enjoy, nor scar,
If any, when on Eastern waves the thunder roars,
    Turn from the storm to these our shores,
Nor would the guinea-fowl enter my belly, nor
    The heathcock of Ionian moor,
With sweeter relish, than the olive picked for me
    From richest branches of the tree,
Or sorrel loving meadows, mallows, too, which heal
    The body burthened with its meal,
Aye, or a lamb slain on the Bound'ries' festive morn,
    Or kid which from a wolf was torn:
'Mid these repasts what joy to see sheep, plump and fed,
    All hurrying homeward to their shed!

Videre fessos vomerem inversum boves
    Collo trahentes languido,
Positosque vernas, ditis examen domus,
    Circum renidentes lares.'
Hæc ubi locutus fenerator Alfius,
    Jam jam futurus rusticus,
Omnem redegit Idibus pecuniam,
    Quærit Kalendis ponere.

To see the weary oxen drag th' inverted plough,
   Their necks with languor drooping low !
And at their posts the slaves, the rich man's household-bees,
   Around the glitt'ring Images ! '
When thus had spoken Alfius, the millionaire,
   Resolved a farm should be his care,
He called in all his money on the Ides, and, when
   The Calends came—*invests again.*

THE END.

Lo! this book has come to an end,
So must you and I, my friend;
If, when comes our judgment-day,
All our good our bad outweigh,
Not unjustly we shall deem
In our favour tells the beam;
Estimate this volume so,
Praise, not censure, you'll bestow.

INDEX OF PART I.

FIRST LINE.	PAGE.
Ah! wherefore will not men take heed	106
Alas! the lost, the dear	14
A little breath of wind, you know	192
Another year has past	35
A preacher to the people spake...	158
Ask we the cause so few	55
As many as the stars which in the Heavens are seen	78
A spotless Lamb by God's command	7
As walking through a wood one sees	145
As when upon seas	165
Before the Lord called Philpotts to his rest	207
Blow, wind; beat, rain	68
Bright green, and then a darker hue	147
Cast, O my soul, aside	81
Come let us to the mountain flee	163
Fountain of Life whose stricken side	122
From the dead carcase of a forest beast	204
God save the Prince of Wales	182

FIRST LINE.	PAGE.
Hail! second Reformation, come at last,	196
Hail, Spirit, last from earth...	11
Hard was his path in life...	202
Head of France, thou didst not well	191
He spake his Royal word	180
High blows the wind and strong the gale...	21
High in the Heavens above	47
How full of comfort is this word	150
If God doth give thee peace	104
In days of trial and distress...	62
In the dark Night, when all is still	42
It was not those who pressed	85
Jesus for ages long concealed	57
Let not the rude unhallowed sound	18
Like to some hidden mine	95
Lilies with your golden hue...	126
Long since has the Orient Sun...	38
Lo! this book has come to an end...	286
Men, brothers bold	23
Methought it was the great dread day	170
Mother with thy precious load...	9
Mourner, weep, to shed the tear	19
Mourn not the saints whose souls have fled	112
Naked as when we left our mother's womb	140
Not St. Govor, but the Lord	130
Oftimes has the Christian soldier	102
O God, we are so weak	81

FIRST LINE.	PAGE.
O Lord, I pray thee to efface	38
O sinner, thou the path of life hast trod	75
O take him away, O take him away	31
Pull hard, my boys, pull hard	189
Rejoice, ye nuptial twain	3
Repine not at sufferings, we need them to prove	108
Restless the waves of human passions swell	41
Say, Colet, say, for whom has rung	198
Seest thou yon engine? Had it not a vent	205
Shifted by every wind that blows	74
Spend life away	148
The armies of the Heavenly hosts	53
The Fury waves her brand of war	190
The Heavenly rest	98
The highest wisdom that this world can give	79
The Lord once said that when we see	161
The Lord who made the worlds above	96
The mercy of the Lord as far exceeds	27
The music of the heavenly spheres	1
These outward things, how much they show	141
The Sun is sinking in the West	40
The sin so small	120
The weapons of the warfare of the Lord	159
The wind it came down with a gusty sweep	72
Think not, O man who dost this book review	1
Think not that babe so weak and small	49
Think not these earthly temples are	110
Think we that man shall lose his meed	93
Those evil humours which oft lurk within	76
Those, only those, are truly blest	61

FIRST LINE	PAGE
Thou wicked weed	143
'Tis said that in the Southern sky	124
To some wild desert glen	100
To the great Cathedral dome	184
Tree that hast weathered many a blast	116
Trust God, pray oft, be ware of sin, and be	207
Upon old Galilee's shore	156
Unfruitful though I be	142
Virgin daughter who art led...	5
We give thee thanks, O Lord	29
What hast thou here	91
What holy secret, Lord, is this	44
What is beauty, what is birth	186
What is the Fatherland	132
What news is there to-day, said one to me	206
When Cain had spilt his brother's blood	87
When Christ was born and laid	51
When God of old did place in Eden fair	114
When God ordained that men	151
When in the wilderness	70
When Jesus came and dwelt on earth of old	154
When on the holy Jesus fell	66
While wandering on my path alone	134
While yet on earth	64
Whoso has lived to threescore years and ten	201
Who that has watched the billows roll	65
Who would not rather for his lot	88
Worthy to live and reign	59
Ye clouds of rain	128
Ye devilish crew	194

INDEX OF PART II.

FIRST LINE.	PAGE.
A sparing and unfrequent devotee	231
Gifts of goblets and bronzes I fain would bestow	271
Happy the man who from all business far away	279
If upward to the Heaven thy hands thou lift	255
Imprisoned Danae brazen tower	245
In light Liburnian galleys thou, my friend, shalt go	275
Mæcenas, sprung from line of ancient kings	211
No ivory nor golden gleam	241
O Faunus, wooer of the Nymphs that flee	251
Offspring of Tuscan kings, for thee	259
O ship, fresh rising billows will bear thee back again	217
Peace asks the man from Heaven in prayer	235
The snows have fled away, now grass comes to the plain	267
Thou shouldst not seek, 'tis sin to know, what end to thee, what end to me	215
What bound to sorrow or restraint should be	227
When that perfidious shepherd was dragging 'cross the sea	221

LONDON:
JAMES WAKEHAM, PRINTER, 4, BEDFORD TERRACE,
KENSINGTON.

www.ingramcontent.com/pod-product-compliance
Lightning Source LLC
Chambersburg PA
CBHW022059230426
43672CB00008B/1227